THE
TWO-INCOME
TRAP

WHY PARENTS ARE CHOOSING TO STAY HOME

SUZANNE VENKER

A POST HILL PRESS BOOK
ISBN: 978-1-68261-478-5

The Two-Income Trap:
Why Parents Are Choosing to Stay Home

Post Hill Press
New York • Nashville
posthillpress.com

Published in the United States of America

For my children, Emma and Henry,
who make everything else pale in comparison.

The greatest reflection of your priorities is your time. Whatever you say about what matters to you, the true test is where you place your time. So if you say your priorities are your partner or your kids or your family or your health, that statement will only be true if your calendar reflects it.

— Nick Crocker

CONTENTS

FOREWORD

Suzanne Venker is helping to lift me out of my growing despair. While my "banging the pot loudly" over the past quarter-century in favor of loving, maritally-committed, two-parent, mom and dad, parent-at-home-when-children-are-home families has seen positive results—I have also witnessed, in horror and disbelief:

- The profound hostility in women's and parenting magazines toward women who raise their own children, not to mention the plethora of articles that support the neglect of children as in the best interest of the child—as long as mommy is happy
- The breakdown of basic, traditional norms, which has resulted in an almost complete loss of a sense of responsibility and obligation apart from one's own self-centered and immediate desires. Feminists disdaining men, marriage, and childrearing helped move women from a place of respect for their femininity and fertility and mothering to a place where shacking-up, out-of-wedlock babies, and daycare practically wiped out their sense of specialness.
- The media in general, and other parents in particular, showing compassionate support and understanding to the oh-so-busy mother or father who accidentally forgot they even had a child because he cooked to death in the

back seat of a car. "It could happen to anybody" is the unbelievable response of other parents.

- The development of products geared to make mothers feel better about abandoning their children to institutionalized daycare for the sake of the mother's well-being: daily charts of when and how much their child pee-ed or pooped and ate and drank, rolled over, or said some words; a camera in the daycare center so the mother can go on her computer and view her child for ten seconds.

This is new-age parenting!

The Wall Street Journal (October 8, 2003) published a book review dealing with the impact of working mothers on the family. "The average two-income family," begins the quotation from the book, "earns far more today than did the single breadwinner family of a generation ago. And yet, once they have paid the mortgage, the car payments, the taxes, the health insurance, and the day-care bills, today's dual-income families have less discretionary income—and less money to put away for a rainy day."

The reviewer points out that "the rush of Mommies into the workplace has had the paradoxical effect of making families less secure, less flexible and poorer." The reviewer also concludes with this telling statement: "But it's weird: The authors know that having a mother at home is economically better for families. They spell it out. Nevertheless, they can't bring themselves to support the reverse migration of America's working Mommies, even if such a thing were possible. 'We remain dedicated to the best part of the feminist movement—the rock-solid belief that women who want to work should have every opportunity to do so.' Yet, if you accept their analysis, you don't have to be a male chauvinist pig to wonder: 'Um, why?'"

I have a great career: I've had a private practice as a licensed marriage and family therapist, sustained a successful radio broadcasting career for a quarter of a century, and written seven *New York Times* bestselling books. I write a monthly column for wnd.com, run a foundation for neglected children, create and hand-craft jewelry to raise money for the foundation, ride bicycles up and down major hills, and took up sailing. Yet I've always been an at-home mother.

The writing happens at 5:00 AM, while everyone is asleep. The radio broadcasting happened first at 10:00 PM, after a full day of childcare, and then shifted to middays while our son was at school. In other words, I squeezed my career in around my mothering and not the other way around. It can be done, if one commits to doing it right—and right means the child does not pay the price for the parent's ambitions and that the parent has the centering and family love that makes life a pleasure.

Once, a young college woman fresh from her women's studies class came to one of my book signings and asked me why I didn't introduce myself with my academic degrees. She said her class talked about me a lot (the teacher was generally insulting), and they couldn't understand why I would identify with motherhood before my accomplishments. I told her that being my son's mother and having him, as a teenager, kiss me in front of his buddies, was my most rewarding accomplishment. I added that I hoped her studies wouldn't warp her to the point that she would not make the choices that would lead her to have a similar reward.

This leads me to *The Two-Income Trap* by Suzanne Venker, who's in her mid-thirties and is herself, right now, making the personal and professional sacrifices that she urges on others. There are hundreds of books explaining why it's acceptable to leave our children in the care of strangers, but very few explaining why we would all be happier if we did not. I am grateful for this book.

Ms. Venker's contribution to humanity, to families, to marriages, to women is huge. In a way, it is sad that she's got to argue points to prove what ought to be a "given." On the other hand, her arguments are beautifully crafted and right on target for today's anti-childrearing atmosphere. My hope for you, the reader, is that after you read this book, you will be unwavering in your commitment to do the right thing, and reap the incredible rewards.

Dr. Laura Schlessinger
2003

NOTE FROM THE AUTHOR

The Two-Income Trap is the updated version of a book I wrote more than ten years ago. It is not politically correct. You will read things here people aren't supposed to say but which nevertheless ring true. Indeed, this book is as much about telling the truth in a culture that wants us to lie as it is about the conflict between children and careers.

I wrote it for three groups of women: (a) mothers who are home with their kids and who need support and validation for the work they do, (b) mothers who are conflicted about whether or not to quit their jobs or whose work-family life has become unmanageable, and (c) women who are not yet mothers but who want to know how they can balance work and family when the time comes.

This book is also for at-home dads. While most parents at home are women, the number of at-home fathers has almost doubled since this book was first published. The reason it centers on women is because that's the way it was originally written, and because I wanted to address the decades-long push to get women out of the home and into the workforce. But the material herein applies to any parent who's home with the kids. So if you're at-home dad, simply substitute the word "dad" for "mom" wherever you see it.

Also, keep the date of its original publication in mind. I've edited the book slightly, but the majority of the content stands as is. In 2002, working motherhood was front and center in the media. Women everywhere were either extoling or lamenting the concept of 'having it all.' Ten years later we're still doing this, which makes the message of *The Two-Income Trap*—that children's needs conflict with adult desires, making it impossible to 'have it all'—as relevant as it was when I wrote it.

Actually, it's even more relevant. According to the United States Census Bureau, the share of stay-at-home mothers rose to 29% in 2012, up from a modern-era low of 23% in 1999. This rise represents the reversal of a long-term decline in at-home mothers that had persisted for the last three decades of the 20th century.

One reason for the turnaround is America's ambivalence about the effects of a mother's absence from the home. Another is women's exasperation in trying to keep up with the demands of full-time work and childrearing. As Anne-Marie Slaughter admits in her explosive 2012 essay in *The Atlantic* entitled *Why Women Still Can't Have It All*, "A rude epiphany hit me: juggling high-level government work with the needs of two teenage boys was not possible."

And then, this: "…the feminist beliefs on which I had built my entire career were shifting under my feet."

Slaughter's article went viral within hours of its posting, and scores of blog posts and articles soon followed. Several women tried to argue the point, but many were grateful to the author for pointing out That Which We Must Not Say: the idea that women can 'have it all'—pursue demanding careers, raise fabulous kids, and remain perfectly sane along the way—is bogus. There are only so many hours in a day. And children, it turns out, need Mom. If Slaughter's article hit any nerve, it was that.

Well, that and the fact that her article was different from what Americans are used to hearing from women like Slaughter. These self-described feminists are forever insisting women *can* have it all "if only" such-and-such would happen. If only men were more like women, if only the government would invest more in childcare and family leave, if only employers allowed parents to leave the office at 5:00 PM, etc. But as this book will explain, the real reason for work-family conflict is far more complex.

Over the past decade, I've heard from scores of women (and men!) who've shared their stories with me. Many have felt the need to justify the most basic human desire: caring for our own babies. Here's a recent email from a woman named Alice:

I was really happy to read that results of verifiable polls are not in line with what the media depicts. I often feel, usually based upon what I see and hear in the media and my limited social contacts (half of whom are dual working couples) that my life choices are absurd. Often it feels I can't relate to most women. None of my former friends gives me the time of day since I quit my lucrative engineering job to stay home with my kids. This just may be natural as they don't have kids yet, but it feels as though somehow I've become a "radical" just for doing something that feels, on every level, natural.

It's all the harder because with my career choice and training, I previously fell under the feminist label; now I just watch in bewilderment. I try to find articles supporting our decision, some kind of encouragement from the world at large, but all I seem to find is study after study showing daycare is fine, that

women should be all about their careers, and that spending
only three hours a day with your kids and eating processed
food is great! I'm being a little facetious, but not entirely. It's
darn hard to find articles praising women for taking care of
their own children.

I've also heard from and spoken to mothers who work full-time and are, quite frankly, miserable. They miss their children terribly, and their marriages have become stressed to the breaking point. But they love their work! What do they do, they wonder. "Is everyone else doing this well, and I'm just not? What's wrong with me?"

There's nothing wrong with you, I tell them. There's something wrong with the arrangement. American families have transitioned from being manageable little communities to bastions of chaos. The two-income family, and by that I mean one in which both parents work full-time and year-round as soon as their family leaves end, is a trap. I call it that because when it comes to raising kids, breadwinning is only part of the equation. The burnout that results from not having someone home to do everything mothers have historically done is huge. That's why high-profile working moms are forever saying they need a "wife."

Well of course they do. What did we think mothers were doing all those years? Eating bon-bons? It is precisely this caricature of the mother at home—that she doesn't do much, or that what she does do can be done by almost anyone—that caused women to flee their homes in search of something more "valuable" to do with their lives. Lack of respect will do that.

Still, few will admit they go to work to preserve their sense of self-worth. Instead they'll insist the dual-income lifestyle was thrust upon them due to the economy. Mothers today "have" to work, they say. And to some degree that's true: we *have* created an economy that demands two incomes to maintain (particularly if you live on either coast). But we did it by insisting mothers couldn't be happy at home. That message came first.

The economics came later. Indeed, all the income growth in the US since 1970 has come from women working outside the home. That is what raised the GDP, making it harder for families to live on one income. And note the date: 1970. That's when feminists began their push to get mothers out of the home and into the workforce. It was a calculated ideological and political move.

The discussion of balance has nothing to do with working-class America. It's a middle- and upper-middle class conversation. Married mothers didn't leave their homes en masse because they were poor—they left because they were pulled in that direction. What women wanted was respect, and the workforce was fast becoming the place to get it. Feminists portrayed the mother at home as a hapless wife who was wasting away her life caring for babies. Let the less educated women do it, they said.

It was this loss of respect, this elitism really, that fueled the dual-income family.

My goal in writing this book was to support women like Alice who find it "darn hard to find articles praising women for taking care of their children." I wanted to highlight the significance of the work mothers like Alice do. I wanted to elevate their status in society. If that upsets parents who don't do what Alice does, so be it. America was—is—saturated in articles, movies, television programs, books, and news stories about working mothers.

Rarely are mothers at home recognized, let alone valued. It's as if they don't exist. Yet they do, and their numbers are growing.

Also, a quick word about the phrase "stay-at-home mom." When I use this term, I'm not actually referring to one type of mother. Yes, some married mothers are exclusively mothers—29% to be exact—but others work out of their homes and vacillate between wearing their work hat and wearing their mom hat, particularly if their children are in school. And many mothers' jobs are flexible, allowing them to be available before and after school.

Of course the younger children are, the less likely mothers are to work full-time outside the home. But even mothers of younger children sometimes work very part-time. Many variables allow for this, which I discuss in the book. Regardless, all of these moms are categorized as "at-home moms" to differentiate them from those who pursue full-time, year-round employment and thus need a constant supply of caregivers on hand.

Even I've never been sure how to define myself. I've been every form of mother: full-time mom; part-time working mom; and somewhat full-time working mom now that both my kids are in school. But I haven't been employed since I was pregnant with my oldest, who's now 14, and my children definitely don't view me as a working mother.

They know I'm a writer, but for years they didn't even know that. My work brings with it the obvious advantage of having no boss, which means everything I do work-wise is tailored around what I consider to be my primary job: raising my kids. As a result, I've never used daycare or hired a nanny, nor have I had the advantage of family help (though that would have been nice!)

Basically, I'm just always around. The downside of my chosen career is my husband and I have less expendable income than the average two-income family. Typically speaking, writers aren't rolling in the dough. At least this writer isn't.

Another thing you may note is the tone of this book is rather severe. My writing has softened a bit over the years, but at the time I wrote it I was hunkered down with new motherhood and feeling rather Mother Bearish about it all. Like millions of other at-home moms, I was tired of hearing myths about my life that were accepted as truth but weren't—like the idea that mothers at home are rich, or that babies and toddlers thrive in daycare.

Both are categorically false. Families with stay-at-home moms are, on average, poorer than those where both parents have incomes. According to the Census Bureau, 75 percent of stay-at-home moms live in households where family income is less than $100,000 per year. And many of these families bring in nowhere near that figure. How we ever came to believe one-income families are wealthier than two-income families is curious. Obviously two incomes, particularly once children are in school and childcare is no longer needed, means more cash in the bank. And babies and toddlers do *not* thrive in daycare, as chapter six will demonstrate.

I was also tired of hearing parents say they "could never be with" their kids all day, as if parents at home love being with children around the clock and have no desire to do anything else with their time. Newsflash: that's not why these parents do what they do. They do it because they feel personally responsible for the care of their children. Or because they didn't have a parent at home when they were young and want a different life for their children. Or because it makes no sense to continue working when the majority of one paycheck goes to daycare. Or because they don't want to miss out on the early years, despite the sacrifices. Or because they want a peaceful lifestyle, not a chaotic one. Or because they believe children deserve a parent at home. The loss of income is, for many at-home parents, beside the point.

* * *

As you might expect, putting these things to paper would prove challenging. After the book's initial publication, I endured the wrath of the media. My original title for the book was *The Work of Motherhood*. However, when authors partner with a publisher they sign away their rights to title their own books; so when my then-publisher changed the title to *7 Myths of Working Mothers*, my heart deflated. I knew a book with that title would fuel the mommy wars, and that was not what I set out to do.

But that is always the result when this topic comes up (though in my case, I couldn't blame people given the new title). Still, my willingness to talk about this subject in an honest and straightforward manner shouldn't have been reduced to "that's the author who thinks mothers shouldn't work." Yet that is how the media framed my message. They knew validating mothers at home would make mothers who aren't home become defensive, so they jumped at the chance to create controversy. We in America have accepted the lie that if you believe in something, you must think ill of those who believe differently. By that logic, no one could support any group or idea because every group or idea has an opposing group or idea! We might as well pack it up and go home.

I didn't write this book to condemn working mothers. I wrote it to condemn the myths and misconceptions about motherhood that many in this group perpetuate. Those are two very different things. I also wrote it to bring a fresh perspective to this debate, and that is this: women *can* have it all, just not at the same time. In fact, the irony of it all is that *The Two-Income Trap* is ultimately about creating a life that incorporates *both* work and family in women's lives. Without the stress. Without the guilt. Without regret.

One of the myths and misconceptions to which I'm referring is the "fact" that most mothers work. Journalists love to report the statistic that "70% of mothers now work outside the home," but they never report the details. "Working mothers," or women who remain employed full-time and year-round after their maternity leaves end, represent *less than half* of American mothers. And most of these women are single moms! That means the number of married mothers who choose to work full-time outside the home and place their children in substitute care, as the women in the media do, is significantly smaller than people think.

The reason the media can manipulate the statistics is because they do not distinguish between mothers who work part-time from those who work full-time. This is a major oversight. It's true if you add the mothers who work both part-time and full-time, you will come up with the 70% figure. But if you combine the half of the 70% who work part-time with America's unemployed mothers, the majority of mothers are still their children's primary caregivers.

These are women who sequence their lives, or move in and out of the workforce to accommodate the needs of their families. They stay home with their kids when they're babies and toddlers and "work" very part-time or out of their homes, and then ratchet up when their youngest starts school. Or they own their own businesses and bring their children to work with them. Or they tag-team with their husbands: she works the day shift; he works the night shift. However it gets done, these women are not working mothers in the way we define the term. Many of these women consider themselves at-home moms.

The distinction is important because it's not most people's perception of the modern mother. And perceptions matter. Most people need social support to feel good about what they do—it's human nature. If it seems as though the trend is to drop one's children off at daycare, more and more parents will begin to get comfortable doing just that. Some of the women you'll read about in this book followed along with what they thought was the "thing to do" and later came to regret it. We never hear from these women, and I think we should.

The great news is that women today have a marvelous opportunity to pursue work and family in piecemeal fashion. Because of the new ways in which we work (self-employment, working from home or at Starbucks, using the Internet or social media to stay connected in the professional sphere) more and more parents—mothers *and* fathers—will continue to create lives that allow them to be "home" with their children, though perhaps not in a traditional manner. And these parents need what they're not getting: respect.

So do children, whose needs haven't changed since the beginning of time. We in America love to talk about "putting children first," which in political terms means throwing more money toward group care, but we're hopelessly dismissive about what children actually need. That information is available (this book included), but the gatekeepers shut down any discussion about children that has the potential to make parents, working mothers in particular, feel bad.

Case in point: Earlier this year, the Pew Research Center released the finding that a record 40% of households with children under 18 include mothers who are either the sole or primary source of income for the family—which in turn sparked a debate about the changing role of women and its effect on children. What the media *didn't* say is that most of these so-called 'breadwinner moms' are single mothers, many of whom rely on welfare. A mere 14% of this group is comprised of married women who are the sole or primary source of income for their families. That's a different message altogether!

But these pesky details present a conflict of interest for female journalists such as Fox News' Megyn Kelly, who was the first to jump on the Pew finding. Kelly's bias was painfully evident as she discussed the research with Lou Dobbs and Erick Erickson. As a full-time working mom of three young children, Kelly was incapable of separating her personal life from the facts. Her defensiveness jumped off the screen, right into viewers' laps.

Bernard Goldberg introduced this problem in his 2004 book *Bias*. In a chapter called "The Most Important Story You Never Saw on TV," Goldberg exposed the clear and overwhelming bias of mothers in the media. "Feminists tend to see any discussion that raises troubling questions about latchkey kids or younger children in day care not as opportunities to learn and discuss something important, but as an out-and-out attack on women and the freedoms they've won since the 1970s."

He adds, "But reasonable people who worry about what's happening to our children aren't calling for a return to the good old days, when women stayed home all day, preferably in the kitchen, preferably baking cookies. One can be in favor of women's advances and still be concerned about the attendant costs. If the media were open-minded, there would be a true debate about this issue."

That's precisely what Lou Dobbs and Erick Erickson tried to do: have a debate, or conversation, about the Pew study. But Kelly talked over them repeatedly (which she's not typically known to do) and labeled the men "judgmental" for simply *questioning* the possible impact of maternal absence. Proving Goldberg right, Kelly shouted down what could have been a reasonable discussion on this very important subject.

The Two-Income Trap exposes this bias and restores respect for the women (and men!) who do the most important and thankless work in the world. I hope you find it enlightening. I hope you find it helpful as you embark on your journey as a parent. I hope, more than anything, it proves at-home parents have nothing to explain—and that they come to believe 150% in the value of what they do.

Suzanne Venker
November 2014

CHAPTER 1

GO AHEAD: LET DOWN THE SISTERHOOD

Women who now leave their families every morning to board commuter trains—the women who have traded in their housecoats for business suits, vacuums for computers, demanding, tantrum-throwing children for demanding, tantrum-throwing colleagues— may well wonder if they haven't simply traded in one form of unhappiness for another. It is at this intimate level that feminism has failed women.

— Danielle Crittenden

If you ask the average person to define feminism, don't expect a long-winded answer. Most people will say it has something to do with the time when women banned together to demand they be treated as men's equals. You know, women's rights and equal pay for equal work—that sort of thing. But chances are, they won't be able to tell you what feminism stands for or what effect it has had because they honestly don't know. And their confusion is valid. After all, there's feminism—and then there's what feminism has become.

Feminism *can* be credited with helping America broaden its views about women and their role in society. I think it's fair to say feminists introduced the fact that women are multifaceted sexual beings whose interests extend beyond the home. Many people also associate feminism with voting rights, though the women who spearheaded that movement were actually called suffragettes. The suffragette movement was about gaining the female vote in all fifty states, which ultimately took place in 1920.

But feminism took a nosedive in the 1960s with three of its major tenets. The first is the idea that women are victims of an American patriarchy hell bent on keeping women down. The second is the idea that biology isn't real, that in the absence of social conditioning men and women would prove to be interchangeable. The third isn't so much an idea as it is a well-orchestrated plan: to get women out of the home and into the workforce. Indeed, it is impossible to overstate the extent to which mothering has been demoted as a result of this powerful political movement.

To be fair, many outspoken feminists lived at a time when women were largely confined to the home. But their historical analysis of why this was so is wrong. Life wasn't this way for women due to large-scale male oppression (which is not to say women never experienced discrimination) but because medicine and technology had yet to offer women the benefit of time. Laborsaving devices such as the washing machine, along with pre-packaged convenience foods and the birth control pill, did more to liberate women from the home than a boatload of feminists could ever hope to do.

Life prior to these advances *was* difficult, which led to some women's frustration and compelled them to speak out. As Christina Hoff Sommers writes in *Who Stole Feminism?*, "American women owe an incalculable debt to the classically liberal feminists who came before us and fought long and hard to gain for women the rights that the men of this country had taken for granted for over two hundred years."[1]

Unfortunately, mixed in with this group of pioneers was an even more vocal group, those who would eventually become the leaders of "women's liberation." Their agenda was far more extreme and would eventually become the boilerplate of modern-day feminism. The basic goal of this group is to persuade women that they're handicapped in every social arena due to their sex. Moreover, these feminists do not wish to hear men's voices at all (unless they support the feminist agenda). Sommers was the first to give a name to this group of women: she calls them "gender feminists."[2]

Gender feminists do not speak for the majority of women. "On the contrary, their divisive and resentful philosophy adds to the woes of our society and hurts legitimate feminism."[3] Gender feminists believe in a different kind of equality, one that goes far beyond reason and common sense. They don't merely argue for a woman's right to choose the course of her own life or for men and women to be treated equally in the workplace. They want men and women to be treated as though they're exactly the same, as though there are no biological differences between them.

But when the feminist movement was in its heyday, its leaders didn't describe their philosophy this way. One of the reasons Betty Friedan, a founder of the National Organization for Women (NOW), won the support of so many women was that her organization appeared merely to support the idea that men and women should be treated equally. And who could argue with that?

What many women didn't realize, couldn't have realized, is that this supposedly simple philosophy would one day wreak havoc on society. For if we make no distinctions between men and women, there can be no accommodation made for the fact that women bear children. And if there were no such accommodation, society could not encourage or support women in the pursuit of at-home motherhood. Every man and woman would be expected to earn an income, and children would not be raised in their own homes by their own parents but would instead grow up in government-subsidized childcare programs or in the care of come-and-go nannies.

And, as it turns out, that's what happened.

But feminists went even further. Despite asserting their platform was all about "choice," it simultaneously belabored the notion that at-home motherhood is not a worthy ambition, that children drag women down, and that women can only find true satisfaction in the workplace. Even now, women's groups state proudly and matter-of-factly that if women want to maintain their true identities, they must be financially independent of men and freed from the shackles of childrearing.

"Women, assert feminists, should treat children as relatively independent appendages to their life of full-time involvement in the workplace. To live what feminists assure her is the only life worthy of respect, a woman must devote the vast bulk of her time and energy to market production, at the expense of children. Children, she is told, are better cared for by surrogates," writes Carolyn Graglia in *Domestic Tranquility*.[3]

This philosophy is most clear in the words of Betty Friedan, who became famous for identifying "the problem that has no name" in *The Feminine Mystique*, which was published in 1963. (An updated version was released in 2001.) The "problem" is the plight of the 1950s housewife: the bored, frustrated mother who can't escape the prison of her home. Most mothers today can empathize with women of that time who felt "stuck." Unfortunately, Friedan's message was not about supporting a woman's choice to pursue a career before or instead of raising a family. It was about encouraging women to leave their children behind in search of greener pastures. It was about demeaning and degrading the work mothers at home do.

Of course, feminists will deny their platform is about anything other than choice. But look at what's happened over the past forty years. In the introductory section of the updated *Feminine Mystique*, Friedan writes that in the 1950s, women were defined solely in terms of their sexual relation to men: "man's wife, sex object, mother, housewife."[4] She writes that this image—which she names "the feminine mystique"[5]—was so widespread that women's magazines, movies, television commercials, mass media, and textbooks all glorified her role in a way that made women who didn't "have an orgasm waxing the kitchen floor"[6] feel alone and aberrant in their desire to get more out of life.

Now compare that image with what we see today in women's magazines, movies, television commercials, mass media, and textbooks: the glorification of the working mother. Almost every television program and commercial today portrays a mother in the workforce. Newspaper headlines repeatedly use the words balance, daycare, family-friendly, juggle and stress to suggest the majority of mothers work outside the home. In other words, the pendulum has swung in the opposite direction.

Now women feel alone and aberrant in their desire to take care of their kids.

"What [feminists] demanded was not a chance to compete fairly but to turn the whole world upside down so as to make it more suitable for them," writes Midge Decter in *An Old Wife's Tale*.[7] It wasn't equality Freidan was after. What she really wanted was to pretend most women don't want to care for children full- time, that most women can be fulfilled only in the workforce rather than at home with their children, where they are "lulled into a false sense of anonymous security in their comfortable concentration camps."[8]

Yet the workforce is not what Friedan said it would be since forty years later, most women still choose to care for their children. "Mothers have not abandoned home and hearth to go to 'work.' The majority of American mothers are still primarily engaged in the oldest economy in the world: the household," writes Ann Crittenden.[9]

This is a surprise to many people, for the media would like us to believe this isn't true. But it is.

* * *

The single greatest problem with the feminist movement is that it was predicated on the notion that women can have it all. As Marlo Thomas said to Phil Donahue in the 1970s, "Men can have it all. Why shouldn't we?"[10] Such an argument could only be made by those who've never done the work of motherhood (and as it happens, Thomas had no children of her own) because once women have done this work, they see for themselves how all-consuming motherhood is. The needs of children are endless.

Part of the problem lay in feminists' assumptions about men. It is simply inaccurate to suggest men have it all. Like today's working mothers, most fathers pursue full-time employment and engage in what we might call peripheral parenting. As former working-mom Tara Fisher observes, "I didn't know my children very well before. I saw them only at their worst time. I would get home at dinnertime. I would cram food into their mouths, and I would put them to bed. I never got to see the good moments, only the tired, cranky ones. Now I get to hear the genuine laughter of being a kid."[11]

Certainly the average father can relate, for he too is used to being away from his children during the important moments of their lives: their first steps, their first words, their first laugh. I'm sure most fathers would rather be present for these milestones than sitting at their desks at work. As one father tells Sylvia Ann Hewlett, "Thinking back on it, I know I didn't have children the way my wife had children. I didn't get to take them out for hot chocolate after school or hang out with their friends. To this day I have no idea what music they like or whether they're afraid of death. I see this as a permanent loss, the price I paid for an absorbing career."[12]

The reality of raising a family is that the parent in the workforce will always be less involved with the children. Which means Thomas and her contemporaries were chasing a dream that none of us, male or female, has ever achieved. Or ever will achieve.

Since the feminist movement first took hold, women have given the concept of 'having it all' their best shot. Thankfully, many have given up. Not only have they experienced what this philosophy has done to children and families, they realize they've been misled. As Lisa Schiffren writes, "My generation grew up accepting the truth of this view; many of us have been surprised to find childrearing so rewarding."[13]

Women have learned several truths about motherhood. First, a mother's identity *is* linked to her children, and working outside the home doesn't change this fact. Second, women miss their children when they're away from them and begin to wonder what is the point of having children if it is not to be with them most of the time. (Isn't this why people have families?) Lastly, women realize their career ambitions have nothing to do with their desire to raise children. Being at home doesn't mean they don't want an independent life, too. They simply recognize a woman's life has seasons, and they're not willing to give this one up.

The concept of choice is always framed in a positive way, but choices can also be a burden. With so much freedom surrounding career and motherhood, so many options for how to proceed, women have a difficult time with whatever decision they make. Peggy Orenstein found in her interviews with over one hundred women across the country that many women are apprehensive about their futures. One woman tells her, "You know, sometimes I wonder if we'd be happier living in a society where there weren't so many choices."[14]

One phenomenon considered a boon for women is the choice to delay marriage and motherhood. This is not an altogether bad idea, but it does have a downside. Aside from the obvious biological implications, postponing motherhood creates a great deal of angst when women decide they are ready to have children. Not only is it hard for them to drop everything they've worked so hard for to pursue something entirely unrelated, they may find themselves wanting to be home with their children and then questioning this most basic desire. This is the true damage of feminism.

I wish I could say this movement has come and gone; but alas, I cannot. Feminists like Friedan are still among us, as Susan Douglas and Meredith Michaels demonstrate in their new book *The Mommy Myth*. The authors claim the state of motherhood has once again resorted to its 1950s ideal: the unrealistic expectation that women can or should be happy at home raising children. The authors are frustrated that women have succumbed to the "idealization of motherhood"—a situation that has occurred, they claim, because of media images that are thrust upon women.

Rather than admit women prefer to be their children's primary caregivers, Douglas and Michaels exhume the message of the feminist movement: "It is important that we remind ourselves of the tyranny of the role of the MRS, because it was what feminists attacked as utterly oppressive, and because, under the guise of the new momism, it has risen, pheonixlike, and burrowed its way once again into the media and into the hearts and minds of millions of mothers."[15]

The tyranny of the MRS. Yikes.

The feminists of today have motherhood all wrong. They're correct that motherhood causes a woman to lose the identity she had prior to having children. But what they do not appreciate, or even get, is that who a woman becomes as a result of being a mother is far richer than who she would have become had she not.

CHAPTER 2

7 MYTHS ABOUT STAYING HOME

*"Mommy, I don't want you to work. Why can't you
be more like Joey's mom? She stays home with him."*

*"Well, maybe that's because Joey's mother can't do
anything else."*

— Judging Amy

"No woman in America today who starts her search for identity
can be sure where it will take her," writes Friedan at the close of
The Feminine Mystique.[1] The year was 1963. And here we are,
forty years later. Just where has the search taken us? Motherhood
has been officially demoted from the top rung of the ladder to the
bottom, and in its place is the all-important career. Women now
spend all of their time and energy—all of it—preparing for a life
at the office rather than for a life at home.

In fact, women's "search for identity" has become so myopic many women forget to *have* children. Nature has to knock on their doors before they realize how much time has passed. And those who manage to conceive, despite their aging eggs, do not bask in their newfound status but instead confront The Big Decision: whether to stay home with their children or return to the workforce.

Most women feel an immediate tug in the direction of home. There is, after all, something magical that happens the moment a baby is placed in our arms. The problem is, society suggests it's unnatural, abnormal even, for a woman to want to take care of her own baby. "Any strong rush of maternal feeling, any desire to surrender pieces of our professional selves, is viewed as a reversion to some stereotype of motherhood the women's movement was supposed to have emancipated us from," writes Danielle Crittenden in *What Our Mothers Didn't Tell Us*.[2]

And so, women begin to question the value of staying home. "Most people, especially young people, need to be confirmed by the community in which they live. They cannot beyond a certain limit establish for themselves a system of their own verities and preferences," writes Midge Decter.[3] As a result, many women jump on the bandwagon, when in truth they would love permission to get off. In other words, today's women are no less conflicted about where they belong than women were forty years ago. Their "search for identity" continues.

Only now the expectations are reversed.

This is perhaps the greatest tragedy of modern America. Because our society encourages mothers to "go to work," women choose to forgo the greatest opportunity of their lives. How sad that any one of us could allow such personal and life altering choices to be governed by an outside force, that we would give up an entire portion of our lives—the most valuable portion of our lives—because we believe what we've been told. Too many women make up their minds about whether or not to stay home with their children even before they become mothers. They don't even consider staying home, as indicated by one of the most popular phrases of the decade: "Oh, I could never stay home full time."

Those who say this make a great assumption, for we can't really know how we feel about something until we've done it. Moreover, this all-too-famous cliché suggests spending a lot of time with one's children is a negative thing. "It amazes me that women say this as though [being with one's children] were a punishment," says one former working mother.[4]

What a woman experiences during maternity leave is but a fraction of what she'll experience over the coming years. That's what happened to Laurie Tennant, who says that her life as a working mother seemed to be working out fine: "I felt perfectly balanced."[5] It wasn't until her second child came, when she was home on another maternity leave, that she had the opportunity to spend a considerable amount of time with her first child, who was by then several years older. She was "jolted by how much she enjoyed the experience."[6] Shortly thereafter, Tennant quit her job.

I remember a conversation I had with a friend of mine who is thirty-six, single, and owns her own business. During the course of the conversation, she mentioned that one of her employees had recently become a full-time mom. She said she was surprised this woman had made the choice to stay home because she did not seem like the "type." I asked her what she meant by this; and she replied, "Well, it's just that she has so much energy that I can't picture her at home all day."

My friend doesn't see the irony in her statement, but this "energy" she assumes is unnecessary is precisely what motherhood demands. As I later pondered our conversation and thought about similar discussions I've had with other women, most of whom were not yet mothers, I realized motherhood is the most elusive profession in the world. It's the one job for which we cannot see the work as it's being done, nor can we assess our progress. Thus, it is impossible to quantify the work the way we do other jobs. As Ann Crittenden writes, "Like the work of a fine seamstress, tiny stitches that build character and confidence are invisible to the naked eye."[6]

All mothers at home know it's futile to convey to the casual observer what their job is like. A woman who does not have children could easily sit with a group of mothers and children and watch as the mothers wipe away a few tears, change a couple of diapers, or discipline their children and wonder what could be so difficult about motherhood. Or she could observe a mother casually walking her baby in a stroller and believe she understands why some women refer to motherhood as "boring."

What she will not appreciate is the work that takes place when no one else is looking. If I were not with my daughter every day, it would be impossible for me to understand exactly how she gains a feeling of self-worth by hearing my voice and seeing my face throughout the day—in the same manner, within the same routine. It would be impossible for me to understand the effect of my presence as she climbs a step and turns to see if I'm there before she moves to the next one. It would be impossible for me to appreciate her ability to make connections between what I say and what I do and how this leads to her intellectual growth. It would be impossible for me to understand how my being there to encourage her to keep trying each time she thinks she can't do something will help mold the person she later will become. It would be impossible for me to appreciate how important discipline is—that it be instilled by the person every day, in the same manner—so she is not confused by the methods of numerous caregivers. It would be impossible for me to understand how vital it is that I am present each day to see that she stays on a routine, eating and sleeping well and avoiding sickness when possible. It would be impossible for me to appreciate how much she needs me when she is sick or tired or sad or bored. Those who are not there every day to see exactly how parenting works can never truly appreciate its value.

Women who want to make an educated decision about whether or not to stay home with their children are entitled to the facts. It's time to debunk the many myths of motherhood that have infected our culture.

Myth #1   Most mothers work.

When you hear a statistic reported on the news, you need to remember that what it means and how it's portrayed are rarely the same thing. The media doesn't sift through the fine print for you. You have to do this yourself, or you'll be misled. But since most people don't have the time or inclination to research the details, they take the media at their word. (If you've heard the term "kool-aid drinker," that's what it means.) And when it comes to motherhood, the media want you to believe, *need* you to believe, that just about every woman in this country is a working mother just like them. But it just isn't true.

Here are the real figures, according to the United States Census Bureau:

For families with children under age eighteen:
Moms employed full-time and year-round: 39.8 percent
   ("working mothers")
Moms employed part-time: 34.3 percent
Moms not employed: 25.9 percent

For families with children under age six:
Moms employed full-time and year-round: 36.3 percent
   ("working mothers")
Moms employed part-time: 37.1 percent
Moms not employed: 26.6 percent[7]

Clearly, the stereotypical "working mother" we hear so much about—the woman who pursues a full-time career and places her children in other people's care—is in the *minority*. The reason the media is able to manipulate the statistics is that they do not distinguish mothers who work ten hours a week out of their homes while their children are asleep and those who work sixty hours a week while their children are in daycare or with a nanny. Thus, the media can report, as *Child* magazine did recently, that "70% of moms"[8] now juggle career and family, because if you add the mothers who work both part-time and full-time, you will come up with this figure.

A mother who brings home an income of even *one dollar* is viewed as a working mother. Since I'm a writer, for example, I'm considered a working mother. That I write intermittently—some days I do, some days I don't, and when I do my daughter is usually sleeping or with her father—is irrelevant. The fact that months or even years could go by before I'm at the computer again is also irrelevant. (This is a work pattern known as "sequencing," a term coined by Arlene Cardozo in her 1986 book of that title.) Despite my sporadic income, and the fact that I do not use substitute care for my daughter, I'm still considered part of the "majority of mothers . . . now in the workforce."

It's also interesting to note the breakdown of our nation's non-school age children. Almost a full 50 percent of mothers is unemployed, and another 12.3 percent is comprised of full-time dads (1 percent), moms who work beside their children (3 percent), and tag-team arrangements (7.8 percent), where mom and dad provide alternate care in different shifts. That means 74.6 percent of non-school-age children under the age of five are in their family's care, while only 25.4 percent are cared for on a full-time basis by someone other than their family. (This alternative care consists of institutional daycare—15.1 percent—in-home daycare—8 percent—and nannies—2.4 percent.) Clearly, these statistics do not confirm the media's image of today's mother.

The result of this myth? Many women assume the majority of children are not being cared for by their mothers and fear that if they choose to stay home they'll be left to venture the seas alone. As Collette Leskovyansky describes it, "I think what the media has accomplished for me is to infuse a sense of despondency about becoming a mother."[9]

Myth #2 Stay-at-home moms have just one mission; working mothers do it all.

These two phrases—"stay-at-home mother" and "working mother"—are the dumbest labels in history. To begin with, all mothers work. The definition of *work* is "the physical or mental effort or activity directed toward the production or accomplishment of something." The dictionary lists a total of thirteen definitions, only one of which refers to money. Clearly there is work we all do—housework, yard work, errand running, exercising—that has no monetary value but still constitutes work. It comes down to what we value.

The problem with the phrase "stay-at-home mom" is that it conjures an image of the 1950s housewife. "If there was any occupation less hip, less relevant, I for one could not imagine what it was. Housewives wore polyester chintz housedresses, baked bundt cakes in their ranch homes, and then drove station wagons to PTA meetings. They were dull, unsexy, fretted over trivialities, and lived vicariously through their husbands and children in order to compensate for their own pathetic incompleteness," writes radio correspondent turned at-home mom Meghan Cox Gurdon. At least, that was the thinking in 1964, "a year after Betty Friedan published *The Feminine Mystique*," writes Gurdon.[10]

And yet, few at-home mothers know anyone who even remotely resembles this caricature: "Wander into any Starbuck's in the hours after the commuters are gone. See all those mothers watching over toddlers at play? If you look past the Lycra gym clothes, the scene could be the 50's, but for the fact that the coffee is more expensive and the mothers have MBAs."[11] There's a huge difference between the average woman in our parents' generation and the average woman today, who has spent years in the workforce prior to having kids. She is therefore no less educated or knowledgeable about the working world than her working mother counterpart.

"[Full-time moms] are not bored, foolish, or frustrated," writes Gurdon. "We wear jeans, miniskirts, and leggings and talk politics as much as we do infant-feeding schedules."[12] The problem is the title: "stay-at-home mom" larks back to a bygone era, when motherhood was essentially thrust upon women. Women today are home by choice, not expectation. And most do not spend their days slaving away in the kitchen, since modern conveniences and mobility have liberated women from being tied to the stove.

The term "working mother" is misleading as well. It conjures an image of a woman who manages a full-time career while performing the work of motherhood simultaneously. She's amazing, we say! Just how does she do it? And of course, she doesn't. She *pays* someone to do the mothering for her so she can focus on her career. She can't, after all, be in two places at once.

Myth #3 At-home motherhood is boring.

There are so many ways to respond to this depiction of at-home motherhood. The first thing that comes to mind is what people mean when they use the word boring. To suggest something is boring implies there's not enough work to do to keep oneself busy, and this is hardly the case with motherhood. The last thing mothers at home are is bored. I can just hear my full-time mom friends now, "I would love to be bored! Bored sounds fabulous!"

If we're referring to the work itself as boring, that's something else. It's true taking care of children all day is not intellectually stimulating. It's hard to read the same book over and over again, or to watch Sesame Street with your kids, or take them to the park for the umpteenth time. But the point is not whether or not this is true. The point is, while *we* may not find these mundane events exciting, children do.

One of the reasons women today refer to being home as boring is that adults now move at lightning speed, so the idea of having to move slowly, as all children do, is challenging. (I discuss this further in chapter five.) Boring, to us, means a lack of stimulation. If we're not constantly running somewhere, we don't know what to do with ourselves. This is unfortunate, for motherhood is our one opportunity to stop the rat race and explore our other talents. At what other point in your life will you have the freedom and flexibility to be your own boss? At-home motherhood offers women complete control of their lives. It's up to us to use it well.

Another problem is the beating sacrifice has taken. The practice of doing for others, of finding personal satisfaction in helping others, is foreign to many people. We've been taught that immediate gratification—whether in the form of a paycheck, a pat on the back, or the ability to do what we want, when we want—is the only way to be happy. But actually the opposite is true. Happiness comes not from focusing on ourselves but from doing for others.

The third reason women refer to at-home motherhood as boring is because too many mothers have fled their homes for the workplace. Had they not, mothers at home would have other mothers with whom to share the experience. It's adult contact mothers crave, and they used to have it when more mothers stayed home. So the more women stay home, the less bored mothers will be.

Finally, there's a truth that lies buried beneath the motherhood rhetoric: children are delightful to be around! (Except when they're not, but that's another conversation.) "Indeed, the dark secret of [motherhood]—the thing that none of us knew until we gave up our paid jobs—is that it's fun. And deeply gratifying," writes Gurdon.[13]

Myth #4 At-home motherhood means domestic slavery.

Well, not exactly. A lot has happened since the days when mothers were scrubbing kitchen floors and making homemade bread. Women no longer slave away in the kitchen, and ironing is all but forgotten. Just about the only thing people have to do to keep house today is know how to work a microwave and push a vacuum.

I thought of this recently when I watched a PBS series in April 2002 called *Frontier House.* Three modern-day families volunteered to live in Montana for five months, replicating life in 1883. It was fascinating. As I sat glued to my chair for three consecutive evenings, two hours at a time, I thought about how impossible it is for any of us to grasp what women of that time had to endure. The typical mother in those days would have to care for her children while doing grueling work.

She would start the stove each morning and tend it throughout the day. She would walk miles to get water. And she would prepare three meals a day using only the most basic ingredients and equipment. This only scratches the surface, but the point is this: we're so far removed from such a life that we've become immune to even the *idea* of hard work. True, this kind of life existed so long ago it hardly seems relevant. But is it? It may be unrealistic to expect us to appreciate the water we come by so easily, but is it too much to expect that we should clean our homes, throw dirty clothes in the washer and dryer and prepare three meals a day without complaining?

We are, in fact, the luckiest women in the world. The kind of labor women used to do, even our own grandmothers and mothers, is foreign to us. I can't help thinking about how any woman over sixty years old must look at our lives and think we're the most spoiled generation they've ever seen. Which, of course, we are. After all, life at home can't get any easier. There should be little left to complain about.

Myth #5 *Mothering doesn't have to mean sacrifice.*

For the past several years, there's been a great deal of material written by women regarding the idea of maternal sacrifice. Some writers insist society thinks "the good mother" is one who happily sacrifices her entire self for the sake of her family and that any woman who doesn't wish to do this is somehow viewed as less of a mother. As Sylvia Ann Hewlett writes, "If young women are to improve their options and widen their choices, they will need to get over this first hurdle: how to combat the attitude so prevalent in our culture that it is somehow unseemly—or greedy—for a woman to want success in more than one sphere of her life. Somehow a woman isn't a woman unless her life is riddled with sacrifice."[14]

I disagree. At no other time in history has it been more acceptable for women to want both work and family in their lives. In fact, it's not only acceptable for women to want this, it's expected. It is rare to find a woman who doesn't want both. The issue is not, as Hewlett suggests, whether women should have interests outside the home, but whether women should make *any concessions at all* for motherhood.

Feminists sold women a bill of goods. They insist women are no more inclined toward sacrifice than men are—and that even if they were, they shouldn't be the ones to make the sacrifices involved in motherhood. But it's a biological fact that women are more nurturing than men and are thus more likely to want to make sacrifices. And fathers make countless sacrifices as well—they're just of a different variety.

Any mother who believes she should be exempt from making sacrifices for her children misses the whole purpose of motherhood. It is only by doing the work ourselves, by making the sacrifices, that we grow as human beings. As Linda Burton writes, "It seems to me that when we are presented with our greatest opportunity for self-revelation and growth, we are presented with an opportunity to come out on top. We may be frightened of mothering. We may not feel up to it, we may run from its challenges, and we may call our fear a simple born ineptitude for the job. But then we will never experience the sea, and we will never see the view from the mountaintop."[15]

Myth #6 Mothers at home lose their identities.

The greatest myth feminists perpetuate is the notion that motherhood causes a woman to lose her identity. That's how Friedan started the conversation, and other feminists love to reiterate the concept. "Mothers should work outside the home. Otherwise, they cannot preserve their identities," writes Joan K. Peters in *When Mothers Work: Loving Our Children Without Sacrificing Ourselves.*[16] Women like Peters have been so successful in preaching this theory that women who are not yet mothers presume they'll suffer this fate and plan on returning to the workforce after they have children.

The discussion of what happens to a woman's identity when she becomes a mother has become far too myopic. Yes, it is true that once upon a time mothers were not expected to have lives of their own and thus sacrificed everything for the sake of their children. And yes, it is true that many children of these women, no matter how grateful they were for the sacrifices their mothers made, wanted their mothers to have "lives of their own." But we've gone too far in trying to make that happen.

In their attempt to seek identities separate from husbands and children, women have sacrificed motherhood altogether. Consequently, children suffer—and so do women, as many come to regret the choices they've made. We allowed our focus on the

Self to cloud our vision of what it means to love others, even, on occasion, at our own expense.

Sacrifice is a reality of life, even for men. Fathers must curtail their own needs in order to address the needs of their families. They may want to play golf every Saturday or go drinking with their buddies every night after work, but they will refrain from doing so if they want a happy family life. They may want to quit their jobs, but they do not have this luxury if they expect to feed their families. Being married and having a family is, by definition, a sacrificial role. Thus, it is only natural that the more sacrifices one makes, the more one's identity (even a man's) gets lost in the process.

But most important is what we don't see about sacrifice: what we gain. Our identities are constantly in flux. Being home with children doesn't cause a woman to be any particular way—it is a woman's personality and attitude that determines her fate. Each one of us has a choice to look at the glass half empty or half full. Just because feminists refuse to look at the glass half full doesn't mean we have to follow suit. And just because some mothers at home—either in the 1950s or today—choose to live their lives through their children, paying little attention to their own needs, does not mean this is an inevitability of motherhood. It is simply a choice some women, for whatever reason, choose to make. Therefore, it makes no sense to say, as Peters does, that all women should become working mothers simply because some full-time mothers are unable to have a conversation about any topic other than their children.

Besides, the reality is that once a woman becomes a mother, her identity *does* become inextricably linked to her children's.

Women simply change when they have children; they are not the same people they once were. Their needs, desires, interests, and world revolve around the needs, desires, and interests of their children, regardless of whether they are with their children throughout the day. "And this is maybe the ultimate irony of her situation: She has gone to work in large part to be free of domestic worries but she is no less consumed by them, even at a distance, encased in her glass tower," writes Danielle Crittenden.[16]

None of this is to belittle the significance of women's careers. Working at job you love is great and important. But it should not define us. As Maria Shriver writes in *Ten Things*, "Even though you may think your job is your life and your identity, it's not and it shouldn't be."[17] As hard as it is to hear, we are all expendable at work.

At home we are not.

Myth #7 A mother who is home with her children wastes her education.

It's a common myth. And perpetuating it, as the character Amy does on *Judging Amy* when she suggests to her daughter that her friend's mom stays home with him because "she can't do anything else," is the mark of true ignorance. For there's no such a thing as a woman wasting her education on motherhood. In fact, quite the opposite is true.

Recent studies have shown, and common sense would conclude, that children who are raised by mothers with advanced degrees and previous work experience have an advantage over those whose mothers do not have such backgrounds. How can you be too educated? Since the work of motherhood is no different from teaching, wouldn't it make sense that a child is at a distinct advantage being raised by an educated mother?

And it's not just children who benefit. The few years we have at home with our children can be the most educational years of our lives as well. It's a matter of how we look at it. If you belabor the fact that the work is monotonous, which it is, and on a level that's "beneath us" as educated women, which it is not (unless you're elitist), you miss the point. Motherhood is an opportunity to impart our knowledge, wisdom, and experience to another human being. The better educated we are, the better educated our children will be.

There's also this. With the exception of low-income families, mothers who return to the workforce almost always provide their children with less educated caregivers. Nannies and daycare providers are not positions commonly sought by women with advanced degrees. Thus, when the educated mother chooses to pursue a career instead of being home with her children, what she invariably tells her children is that her education and abilities are so superior that to stay home to pass this knowledge and intellect on to them would be a complete waste of time.

* * *

The genesis of these myths lies in the feminist movement, whose founders had little regard for motherhood. Over the years, the pressure to conform to feminist ideals became palpable. What many don't know is how emotionally troubled most high-powered feminists are and how they lash out at society as a result.

Betty Friedan all but admits it: "I almost lost my own self-respect trying to hold onto a marriage that was based no longer on love but on dependent hate. It was easier for me to start the women's movement than to change my own personal life."[18]

Rather than face her own demons, Friedan lashed out at society (men, employers, the government) and blamed *them* for her discontent. Other feminists followed suit. But these women do not represent the majority of American women. The only reason the myths prevail is because they're espoused by some of the most powerful voices in America. Who are they?

Let's begin with gender feminists. This group has not only been vocal in the political arena and with public policy, they've written scores of books and articles that glorify the two-income family. Gender feminists believe children should never interrupt the trajectory of a woman's career. Women must be happy, above all else; so if mothers feel they need to be career women, that's fine. Children don't *need* their mothers anyway—they can thrive in daycare, given the right setting. These are women who believe mothering one's children is a matter of choice, not responsibility. Betty Holcomb, author of *Not Guilty! The Good News for Working Mothers*, even subtitles one of the chapters in her book "The Myth of Personal Responsibility."

Furthermore, they add, if women feel insecure about their decision to return to the workforce, that has nothing to do with them. The only reason they're hesitant is because husbands and employers are unsupportive of mothers who work. (An absurd claim since today's husbands have no voice if they want their wives to stay home, and employers have gone out of their way to support working mothers.) They're convinced society ostracizes mothers for their career ambitions and expects them instead to be the Perfect Mother. This is why mothers feel guilty about leaving their children every day: they're victims.

Susan Chira, author of *A Mother's Place: Choosing Work and Family Without Guilt or Blame*, took a six-month maternity leave (from her job as deputy foreign editor at *The New York Times*) that she found to be "oppressive" and "boring."[19] She describes her first year of motherhood as being nothing like what some of her friends experienced or what she imagined it to be. In describing the moments with her daughter, she writes, "There were moments of ecstasy: staring at her hands sketching balletic movements in the air; the weight of her soft, warm body when she drifted to sleep on my chest; her first laugh. But I was drowning."[20]

Apparently the sacrifices involved in caring for a newborn got the better of Chira, so back to work she went. But not before writing a book that purports to absolve working mothers of any guilt and blame. Rather than admit she couldn't handle the job, which would have been far more admirable, she writes that "sacrifice has no place in the motherhood pantheon,"[21] and then justifies her decision to return to the workforce by creating falsehoods about mothers and children, such as the idea that mothers and children can be apart for hours or days with no ramifications. Or that daycare is perfectly fine for children as long as its quality is high.

But no matter how many myths women like Chira come up with to make themselves feel better, it is overwhelmingly obvious they return to the workforce for one reason: it is the easier job. That's the other big secret about why mothers work. A woman I know recently told me her working mom friends tell her each time they have another baby how they can't wait to get back to work after maternity leave ends so they can "have a break." What drives these women, perhaps, is the *idea* of being a mother, not actually being one. Perhaps it's the coming home at the end of the day and being lavished with love and attention that matters. As one woman tells Peggy Orenstein, "I want to have kids, I just don't want them in my life."[22]

Sociologist Arlie Hochschild was the first to identify this group of women in her book *The Time Bind: When Work Becomes Home and Home Becomes Work*. Her groundbreaking study revealed the truth about mothers who work: many flee the pressures of home for the ease and orderliness of the workplace. As one woman tells her, "I always tell people here that I come to work to relax. I know to some people this sounds mean, but to me it's eight hours of relaxation. I can go to work and the kids aren't right in front of me to worry about. At work, I can do more of what I want. At home, I have to do what the kids want."[23]

In 1997, an article in *U.S. News and World Report* entitled "Lies Parents Tell Themselves About Why They Work" exposed this truth as well. It outlined the reasons parents give for choosing to work and explained the discrepancies in their claims. The theme of the article is similar to Hochschild's: that despite people's excuses, the truth is that some parents would simply rather be at work. It gives parents permission to avoid their responsibilities. "The lies parents tell themselves—combined with the fraudulence of the public debate—make it difficult to devise reform or change in attitudes in a way that might ease pressures on families."[24]

To sell their anti-motherhood message, gender feminists rely on their friends in the media. That's the group with the real power. While journalists cannot say outright—as their gender feminist friends can—that mothers *should* work outside the home, they still manage to convey the message that few women stay home with their kids anymore. They also focus on issues related to daycare, guilt, stress, and balancing work and family as though their audience is a replica of them.

But the one subject the media won't discuss is the one that really matters: the children. "The elite journalists in network television don't report the really big story—arguably one of the biggest stories of our time—that this absence of mothers from American homes is without historical precedent, and that millions upon millions of American children have been left to fend for themselves with dire consequences," writes Bernard Goldberg.[25]

And the reason the media won't report this story is because "elite journalists" believe Americans think as they do about motherhood. Those in the media see their views as "sensible, reasonable, rational views."[26] In their minds, a good and just society would accept the idea that children don't need their mothers.

But the only way to be truly fair when it comes to this subject (and thus prove ourselves to be a good and just society) would be to look at the issue holistically. That means studying the negative effects of daycare and including in our discussion the voices of at-home mothers, daycare workers, and teachers. That will never happen of course, for America's minority—those powerful voices that emanate from our televisions—are not the reasonable people they think they are. To them, this subject can only be discussed in positive terms, which means information can only be gathered by those who have a vested interest in daycare being a *good* thing. To do otherwise would mean facing truths about their lives they'd rather not.

And so, because the most powerful voices in America refuse to address the scope of modern motherhood, our society never gets to the heart of the matter. Instead we just dance around it. "Of all the explosive subjects in America today, none is as cordoned off, as surrounded by rhetorical landmines, as the question of whether and just how much children need their parents—especially their mothers. The subject is essentially off-limits for public debate," writes Mary Eberstadt.[27]

The most powerful voices in America aren't interested in truth at all, and they're certainly not committed to children. The only thing they're committed to is "choice." So rather than having an honest and fair public debate about kids and careers, they choose to convey the message that not having mothers at home is normal and good, even something to which women should aspire. They choose to tell America this trend is here to stay and that balancing work and family is a perfectly workable lifestyle for women. Just as Friedan wrote that women in the 1950s were defined "solely in terms of their sexual relation to men,"[28] today's women are defined solely in terms of their careers.

This, say the most powerful voices in America, is progress.

CHAPTER 3

THE TWO-INCOME TRAP

Many women must work because of material needs, but such needs do not begin to account for our contemporary rate of maternal absence.

— *Mary Eberstadt*

Rarely will a mother admit she holds on to her career because she feels that without it she has no identity, nor will she admit that society has had any influence on her decision. But then she may not be aware of it. Trends are enormously powerful: they sink into our subconscious without our knowledge. It isn't until years later that we look back and say to ourselves, what was I thinking? It's like fashion. Each decade there's a particular hairstyle or clothing style that's considered "in." We're convinced it looks terrific. But have you ever looked back at, say, the 1980s and seen what we thought looked terrific? It's downright scary.

Cultural trends are no different. All of us are influenced by what we see and hear around us—that's why television is so powerful. The media depend on our being influenced by their messages; it's how they make money. But imagine, for a moment, how you might behave differently—or even think differently—if there were no such thing as television. Pretend you live in the 1920s or 1930s. How do you think your views about motherhood would be different if the only contact you had with the outside world was your family and friends?

Just think about it a second: you've never seen television before in your life. Now imagine you're pregnant and about to have a baby. What do you think your reaction to motherhood would be? My guess is that unless you were in financial straits, it wouldn't occur to you that you had a choice about whether or not to take care of your baby.

Today, the media is constantly there to remind women they have a decision to make. "Many women have been seduced by the siren calls of feminist theorizing. Some of us have come to believe that our self-esteem depends upon our jobs and that childcare is mind numbing, spirit-killing drudgery. These are not necessarily statements that women would come up with spontaneously, in the absence of feminist tutoring," writes Jennifer Roback Morse.[1] The decision to become a "working" mother or a "stay-at-home" mother, then, is a distinct cultural trend. It is the reason every pregnant woman is now asked, "So are you going back to work?"

But those who do decide to go back to work are not comfortable telling people they work because they want to. So they've come up with a more acceptable reason: money. Never mind that America is wealthier than ever and that the modern generation is the most spoiled in history. According to popular belief, most mothers today work because they "have to." In the meantime, the truth—that many mothers would rather be at the office than home with their children—lies buried in our social conscience. That is why women feel a burning need to tell people they work for financial reasons. They would rather claim to be among the minority of women who have no real choice in the matter than admit they don't want to stay home.

That's not to say all working mothers knowingly misrepresent themselves. There are many mothers who really, honestly believe they have to work. But the reason they do is not that we live in shaky economic times but because today's generation has grown up with every possible comfort and convenience. They've never faced war or a depression; they've never had to save their pennies and wait until Christmastime to get that one special thing they want; they've never been told they couldn't buy something because they didn't have the cash; they've never been told to walk or ride their bikes somewhere because there was no available car; they've never had to wear the same outfit two days in a row; they've never had to cook from scratch and make do with whatever's in the pantry; and they've never had to clip coupons. Today's generation has become so accustomed to an easy life they have no idea how to live any other way.

The belief that mothers 'have' to work suggests women who stay home with their children are among the small, fortunate group of women who are able to do so. "You're so lucky—I wish I could afford to stay home" is a common refrain mothers at home are forced to hear. This group is constantly being reminded that the only reason they can be home with their children is because they're rich. "The question we ought to be asking is why, in the space of a generation, we have come to consider taking care of our own kids—even if it's just for the few short years before they are in school—as a perk of the rich, like yachting?" writes Danielle Crittenden.[2]

But times have changed, people say. In our parents' day, things were more affordable. This argument rests on the "soaring costs of housing and college tuition, but even those expenses have not risen fast enough to explain the massive entry of women into the workforce," write Shannon Brownlee and Matthew Miller.[3] The average new home has "38% more square footage than in 1970," so it's not as though we're spending more money than our parents did for the same house. We simply have higher expectations.

Take the neighborhood I grew up in. Thirty years ago, the houses were considered sizable (averaging about 2200 square feet), and each house had a good-sized yard. The neighborhood is also very attractive and in a good location. Today, almost every young couple that has moved into the neighborhood has doubled the size of their home. Clearly, what we deem to be affordable isn't what people in previous generations considered affordable. In addition, while the elite private colleges "have soared at nearly twice the rate of inflation in the past two decades, nearly 80% of students attend public colleges, and their average is only $2,800 a year."[4]

The real problem is we can't put our wealth in perspective. David Brooks talks about "the psychology of abundance" in an article in the *New York Times* Magazine. The abundance of wealth "really does seep into your soul," he writes, causing us to be careless and casual with our money. As a result, "life becomes a vectorial thrust toward perpetual gain and aspiration fulfillment. It takes a force of willpower beyond the call of most ordinary people to renounce all this glorious possibility."[5]

That is precisely the reason we refer to at-home mothers as lucky—because the alternative is to believe these women are somehow able to "renounce" that second income, that they're able to live without abundance. But the only reason we view it this way is because we've lowered the bar for what constitutes a need. Our "needs" have come to mean six-figure salaries, vacation homes, a third car, and a housekeeper. Anything short of that and we're in the poor house.

But we're already rich without these things. "If one's family income is somewhere near the $75,000 mark, "you probably make more than 95% of the people on this planet. You are richer than 99.9% of the human beings who ever lived. You are stinking rich," writes Brooks.[6] Hence, to suggest at-home mothers are lucky is absurd. These women are home because they'd have it no other way, regardless of their financial status. (In fact, most American families in which the mothers are home full-time are *not* wealthy.) Being at home with one's children has little to do with how much money a family makes and everything to do with how people choose to live. Their quality of life is more important than the extra income.

Indeed, most families in which mothers are home live modestly by today's standards. They do not employ housekeepers, drive fancy cars, go on expensive vacations or shop indiscriminately. (But I would certainly agree the minority of mothers who stay home and *do* live this way are lucky!) They are families who know how to budget, the way people used to do. Nevertheless, our society readily accepts the notion that it takes two incomes to make ends meet. "It is pathetic that in the year 2001 we have to remind people that two incomes are necessary for basic survival in most families," writes Peggy Orenstein.[7]

Basic survival? In the twenty-first century? I don't think so.

Few people today, at least those of us born after 1960, have any idea what basic survival means. Too many parents convince themselves they 'have' to work because they don't know how to live on a budget. It makes perfect sense that these parents would assume mothers at home are fortunate or even rich. Otherwise, why else would they be there? They couldn't possibly *choose* to live on less, so they must be wealthy. "It's easy to get addicted to a certain standard of living, and to make all other lifestyle decisions based on the assumption that both parents have to work full-time," writes Stephen Covey in *The Seven Habits of Highly Effective Families*. "The point is that there are options, there are choices."[8]

Like canceling cable. Or going out for lunch instead of for dinner. Or not going out at all and cooking in your very own kitchen. Or ironing your clothes rather than taking them to the dry cleaner. Or making lunch instead of buying it. Or making gifts instead of buying them. Or having dates with your husband that don't require spending a lot of money. Or keeping the same car for ten years. Or using cloth towels instead of paper towels. Or checking books out from the library instead of buying them from a bookstore. Or not buying your kids a lot of toys they'll never use. Or only going on one vacation every other year. Or living in a smaller home. Or having simple birthday parties at home rather than renting a place. Or only buying clothes you need rather than clothes you want. Or canceling your gym membership and going running instead. Or sharing babysitting duty with your friends rather than paying for a sitter.

The point is, if your goal really is to be with your children, you'll find a way to make it happen. Luck has nothing to do with it. Countless books have been written to help people learn how to live on one income. The information is available for anyone who wants to take advantage of it. And there's never been a better time to get more for our money. With the fierce competition that exists today, there's no reason to pay full price for anything. For the first time ever, consumers don't have to sacrifice quality for paying less.

* * *

There's no end to the steps a family can take to have a parent at home. Take, for example, those who live in areas such as New York or California where the standard of living really is high, so much so that a person could argue that two incomes are necessary to make ends meet. That this is true does not preclude women from having options. If being home with one's children is the priority, a family can always move to a more rural area or even to a different city.

When I was in my mid-twenties and married to my first husband, we lived in the New York area. Although we did not have children, I was concerned the lifestyle and high cost of living would not be conducive to a healthy family life. He didn't agree.

Needless to say, it's not a coincidence I now live in the Midwest where things are more affordable and where the quality of life is much better for raising a family. I knew I would miss New York—and I do, very much—I just wasn't willing to compromise when it came to my future family. As Covey writes, "The place to start [in seeking a work and family balance] is not with the assumption that work is non-negotiable but with the assumption that family is non-negotiable."[9]

Until we are able to do this, we will continue to convince ourselves that most mothers today 'have to work.' And the media must do its part by not supporting the idea that most families today require two incomes to get by and are in desperate need of childcare, particularly when there's plenty of research to prove otherwise. As Brownlee and Miller observe, "Better-off Americans are nearly as likely to say they work for basic necessities as those who live near the poverty line."[10]

If it were true that most families could not survive on one income, then why, as we learned in chapter two, do 60.2 percent of married-couples with children below age eighteen have either a non-employed mother or a mother who works only part-time? It's also interesting that those who work to make ends meet have no problem admitting that having a mother at home is best, while those who work by choice do everything in their power to dispute this fact.

Mothers who want to be home with their children but cannot be are *not* the women who tout the benefits of daycare or suggest their children are better off with someone else during the day. It is only those who work by choice that insist their children are thriving in daycare, or they wish they could afford to be home with their children. These parents create a litany of rationalizations, and for good reason. As Midge Decter writes, "Those who work, not from stark necessity but out of the need in some fashion to make their way in the world, suffer from the pinch of insecurity about the effect on their children of the choice they have made. Such is the inevitable price of worldly ambition."[11]

There's more. The assumption that it takes two incomes for most families to make ends meet suggests having two incomes is always advantageous. But many families discover a second income is not advantageous at all. In fact, it can actually cost to work. The money from a second income—unless it's a six figure salary—will be eaten up by commuting costs, child care, eating out, work attire, dry cleaning, convenience foods, and, of course, taxes. By the time you add all that up, there isn't much left. Indeed, the Census Bureau reported in 1997 that the difference in the median income level of married-couple families with children below the age of eighteen in which both the husband and wife work "year-round and full-time" and families in which only the husband worked was $17,638. Subtracting work-related costs, you will find that the average two-income family nets perhaps several thousand dollars a year, to say nothing of the cost of time (the focus of the next chapter), which is immeasurable. There is little net gain to a second income.

It's amazing, when you think about it, how much value we place on money. I'm reminded of an interview Matt Lauer of the Today show did with the actress Julianna Margulies of ER fame. Lauer asked Margulies about her decision to leave the show, and she said she had done all she could do with the character and that it was time for her to move on. Lauer then mentioned the show had offered her some "ridiculous sum of money" to stay, and he wanted to know how she could possibly walk away from that kind of money. Margulies smiled and explained that she had already made a great deal of money and that there were other projects she wanted to pursue.

But Lauer wasn't satisfied. He looked at her as though she were crazy. How can you not stay just one more year so you can get that salary, he asked. Margulies was forced to repeat her answer. We are so damn materialistic we can't appreciate why a person would walk away from even more millions of dollars than she already has.

Money can actually add to one's problems, for the more money one has the more money one has to manage. And the more money there is to manage, the more complicated things become. And the more complicated things become, the more potential there is for conflict. Indeed, wealth can cause as much strain as can the struggle of never having enough. We don't need as much as we think we do. The only reason we think we do is that people are continuously looking at what their neighbors have. If they could resist this temptation, they might find that they have a great deal more than they think.

None of this is to suggest we should be happy living on bread and water or that one should never partake of the finer things in life. On the contrary, my tastes are as extravagant as the next guy's. And there's nothing wrong with being successful or wealthy! But the fact remains that when people have more money than they know what to do with, particularly if they've never known any other way of life, they tend not to appreciate life's small pleasures.

Even the big pleasures become no big deal since they can indulge themselves whenever they want.

That's one of the reasons wealthy people are susceptible to discontent. There really *is* such a thing as having too much. As the Dalai Lama tells Oprah in the August 2001 edition of *O, The Oprah Magazine*, "When you are discontent, you always want more, more, more. Your desire can never be satisfied."[12] And so it is with money. It has the ability to fulfill our material desires but can deplete us in every other way that matters.

And it has. In Robert Reich's book, *The Future of Success*, he writes that in 1961, 41 percent of college graduates said, more than anything else in the world, they wanted financial success. In 1998, that number jumped to 78 percent. Our desire for success is palpable, and our ambition has paid off: our economy is stronger than it has ever been.

But here's the clincher. Reich explains that by becoming wealthier, one would assume we could afford ourselves more time for the more important aspects of our lives, such as our family, friends, and our selves. But, in fact, the opposite has occurred. The wealthier we become, the less time we devote to our lives outside of work. The less time we spend with our families. He writes that the question we should be asking ourselves is, "Would we choose this new reality if we fully appreciated its consequences for the family life we might otherwise have? In other words, is this new economy worth what it costs us?"[13]

One would hope that the answer is a resounding "no." Unfortunately, today's generation sees the world through a very different lens than previous generations. We are by far the most privileged group in history. We travel, shop, eat out, and spend money we don't have. Even the everyday things technology has given us do not seem superfluous but necessary—part of our "basic survival."

And we had luxuries even before these technological devices! As Anna Quindlen writes in *A Short Guide to a Happy Life* (paralleling Brooks' "psychology of abundance" theory), "Those of us who are 2nd and 3rd and 4th generation are surrounded by nice cars, family rooms, patios, pools—the things our grandparents thought only rich people had. C'mon, let's be honest. We have an embarrassment of riches. Life is good."[14]

Some people believe that since we've never experienced the financial hardships that people in our parents' generation did, we're somehow better off. But we've only traded one problem for another. We may be more comfortable than our parents were and struggle less with day-to-day living, but what we've lost is far greater. When we're never forced to do without, or when we never have to make a choice between two things, or when we shop at will regardless of whether we need or can afford something, we lose sight of what matters.

And somewhere, deep down inside, we know this. After all, we inhale books and movies that teach us about the meaning of life, the stories in which a man is lying on his deathbed and his wife sits next to him, realizing that she would trade in all her worldly goods to have him back. It seems that the things we value most in this life are only appreciated after they are taken from us. This is why doing without can be so valuable.

Unfortunately, sacrifice and discipline are not qualities that are taught or encouraged in today's society. Take credit cards, for example. They've been around forever, but they've only recently been abused. Indeed, the credit card debt of today's average household is $8,367. "Just because I don't have cash for something doesn't mean I shouldn't buy it," says Jen Rinkes, twenty-nine. "I don't think debt is a sin," she adds. "I'm living in a style I want to become accustomed to."[15]

Because of this philosophy—the "I must have everything I want right this very minute" approach—many women are unable to see the big picture, particularly when it comes to motherhood. Less is actually more. A second income may provide their families with more things, yes, but this doesn't necessarily make the family better off. As Gregg Easterbrook points out in his recent book, *The Progress Paradox*, while the average American's income has doubled in the last fifty years, the percentage of Americans who describe themselves as "happy" is half of what it was. It stands to reason, then, that once we have our basic needs met, having more money often means only having more money to spend. And this has very little to do with improving the quality of family life.

On August 21, 2001, Oprah introduced Ric Edelman, author of *Ordinary People, Extraordinary Wealth*, who explained the difference between wants and needs and proved the concept of "less is more." He said that when people get bogged down with excess, they often get caught up in aspiring for more (as the Dalai Lama said). The only way to gain clarity, then, is to scale down one's lifestyle. Then Oprah introduced Bill and Melissa, a couple that had a great deal of debt. Bill makes $41,000 a year, and Melissa is a full-time mom. In order to get out of debt, they cancelled cable TV, got rid of their cell phone, and began cooking meals at home rather than going out to restaurants. They also used the library rather than purchasing books. The result? They saved at least $6,000. What's more, they found that the time they spent together in the kitchen brought them closer together as a couple. It allowed them to share the household duties, talk with one another, and enjoy a creative process. Bill and Melissa are a textbook example of how less really can be more.

Thomas J. Stanley and William D. Danko discuss this same idea in their book *The Millionaire Next Door*. "Most people have it all wrong about wealth in America. Wealth is not the same as income. If you make a good income and spend it all, you are not getting wealthier. You are just living high. Wealth is what you accumulate, not what you spend."[16] Stanley and Danko should know. They studied the lives of America's most wealthy (defined as people whose net worth exceeds one million dollars) and found that the underlying factor in their wealth was the ability to shun the superficial trappings of a high-consumption lifestyle: expensive clothes, flashy cars, enormous homes, and the like.

Instead, these families—particularly the self-made millionaires—tend to live well below their means. They are people who understand the value of a dollar, often because many of them have lived through hard economic times. To these families, money represents security. Today's generation, on the other hand, hasn't had the "advantage" of living through hard economic times, so money represents something very different: buying power. And therein lies the problem. For once we get a taste of the good life, as people have today, it's almost impossible to go back. As my father used to say, "It's much easier to go up in one's standard of living than it is to go down."

It's time to stop making money the scapegoat. Raising children is a choice, not a luxury. Everything we do in life is a choice.

"We're always making a choice, although we may prefer to deny that we have choices; we might not want to accept the trade-offs they imply," writes Reich.[17] And except for the very wealthy, the choice to have children will always mean having to give up some things. Maybe even many things. And the fact that our society won't embrace motherhood despite this fact says a lot about who we are. But if there is any ray of light in the dark period surrounding the events of September 11th, it is perhaps a greater appreciation for our values.

Even the media changed its tune for a while after September 11th. They discussed whether or not things like money and power still seemed important. "Across every nation, at nearly every level of the workforce, a subtle but far-reaching shift in priorities is under way. Values that were pre-eminent for many people—career, status, money, personal fulfillment—are now taking a back seat to more fundamental human needs: family, friends community, connectedness with others," writes Sue Shellenbarger in *The Wall Street Journal*.[18]

If this is true, then what we should be seeing is more mothers (or fathers) quitting their jobs and going home to raise their children. Let's hope they do. Let's hope women begin to put motherhood into perspective and come to see its value, despite the sacrifice. A former working mother, Linda Burton writes, "Somehow, after the unparalleled experience of knowing children, goals like money and power and prestige have a lot less appeal."[19]

Indeed they do.

CHAPTER 4

THE FALLOUT

What kind of example do we set as we race from here to there, trying to accomplish more, have more, experience more? When I am feeling rushed, overworked, and stressed, that quality seeps into the very air around me. In a society that endorses activity, I think we would all do well to put more trust in stillness.

— Katrina Kenison

Just about the only time it's considered acceptable to spend a lot of time at home is during the holidays. During the holidays, people expect that we'll be holed up in our respites, away from work and all other distractions. We read; we bake; we listen to music; we spend time with our families; we phone our friends and loved ones; we even promise ourselves that we will do more of these things in the New Year. Then the New Year arrives, and we return to the only life we know: work. Work is now our reason for living, and home is almost superfluous.

Admittedly, we cannot blame this new way of life solely on feminists kicking women out of the home. Despite their influence, technology has accelerated all of our lives. But rather than enjoy the time we've gained from these technological advances, we've used them to become twice as productive. Because of this, productivity is now the focal point of our lives, while doing nothing in particular—just hanging out with our kids—is considered a waste of time.

"Thirty-eight percent of Americans feel they "waste" their leisure time if they don't accomplish something productive," writes Sue Shellenbarger in *Parade* magazine.[1] And yet it is within this chronic need to *be* productive that we never really *are* productive. We spend all our time running from Point A to Point B rather than being successful at any one thing, rather than living life at all.

We are virtually handicapped outside of work. The moment we do have a minute to ourselves we pick up some technological device rather than find creative ways to be productive. And in this age of overindulgence, of progress and self-fulfillment, our children have followed our lead. They've become us. As Judith Regan writes in *O*, "'Mommy, I'm bored,' my daughter announces after a day of video arcades, Rollerblading, eating out, and instant messaging her friends. She is, at age 9, bored to death while being bombarded by stimulation."[2]

Despite all our supposed advantages, we are discontent, we get bored easily, we complain about a lack of time, we're always in a hurry, and we're constantly looking for things to be bigger or better. We have the opportunity to lead more fulfilling lives than previous generations, yes. But we've chosen not to take advantage of it.

Don't get me wrong. I'm thrilled to be living in the postmodern era—I'm just not thrilled to be living in a society that allowed our progress to change who we are. Here again, previous generations had the advantage. They may have had to wash and make their clothes by hand and live without microwaves, televisions, and computers, but at least they felt a sense of pride and accomplishment for their hard work. At least they made good use of time. At least they valued their homes and children more than they did their jobs.

Where we once coveted the comfort and security of home and family, as well as honoring the work that went into making a home, we've now turned our attention to the world of work, to paid labor. Psychologist Ilene Philipson writes about this transformation in her book *Married to the Job*, suggesting we're a nation obsessed with work and that life outside of work has become unfulfilling.

Philipson describes the difference between her generation and today's: "Growing up in America after the Second World War, I was part of a social movement that eschewed paid labor and embraced leisure time. Hanging out, that is, unstructured time, time to spend with friends, time to reflect, wonder, and muse, was an overriding goal. Creative work—baking bread, gardening, engaging in traditional forms of art like painting or playing music—and working to make a difference in the world, were highly valued."[3]

Such values are no longer an "overriding goal." The goal now, writes Philipson, is not just to meet our financial needs through work but our emotional needs as well. Work, not family, is where we find meaning and a sense of accomplishment. Work is where we feel appreciated, where we find our identity. But it's not working. That's because we can never replace what we're missing at home with what we find in the workplace. The workplace is about money and success—family is love, connection, and personal growth. This is where at-home moms get shortchanged. "We value and admire the adult who spends his or her life living alone, working long hours, more than the individual who cares for others at home."[4]

This was not the case in the past, but today we measure our worth according to our ability to work long hours and become wealthy in the process. Our need to keep up with the Joneses is palpable. Which is why, although technology could afford us more leisure time, we choose instead to live an accelerated lifestyle. "We may very well have an hour more than we did 30 years ago, but we're moving at a much faster pace, which leaves us feeling stressed," writes Karen Levine in *Parenting* magazine.[5] She adds, "Theoretically, the purpose of leisure time is to offer psychological renewal from work, but when we spend our leisure hours at the same kind of frenetic pace as our work hours, we emerge feeling drained."[6]

And it's our choice of activities that work against us. Previous generations would spend their leisure time playing cards and games, or talking, reading, and making scrapbooks for their children. They would put photo albums together, read novels, write letters to their friends, and take long walks. We do none of these things. Just about all of our free time is spent in front of the television or running errands while we talk on our cell phones or shopping for no particular reason, except that we're bored.

This desire for things to be bigger and better doesn't make families stronger. It weakens them. Televisions, computers, cell phones, email, beepers and the Internet keep us from being productive and connected to one another. They keep us from doing things we can feel good about—things like reading, sewing, carpentry, gardening, cooking, writing, and playing games with our children. Such activities allowed previous generations to lead richer and more fulfilling lives.

Our idea of a rich, fulfilling life means work, work, and more work. It means running through life, full speed ahead. And we give no thought whatsoever to what gets lost in the process. As Laura Pappano says in an interview about her book *The Connection Gap*, "In spite of our ridiculously full lives, it all doesn't add up to what it's supposed to. We're doing all this stuff, but we're not feeling it; it seems to wash over us."[7] This is why, no matter how hard women try to squeeze children in around their hectic career lives, the result will always be chaos.

And in the midst of all the chaos, motherhood, too, washes over us.

* * *

American Heritage's definition of the word *balance* is "a state of equilibrium or parity characterized by the cancellation of all forces by equal, opposing forces, and a harmonious or satisfying arrangement or proportion of parts or elements." It is impossible for any parent who works full-time to achieve balance because the amount of time they spend at work is entirely out of proportion to the time they spend with their children. "We can't be fully at home and fully at work at the same time. Work and life don't overlap so much as they collide or intersect, leaving us to sit in our ergonomically correct swivel chairs and pivot between the two. And each time we turn toward one, we are, in that moment, turning away from the other," writes Lisa Belkin in *Life's Work*.[8]

Indeed, not one of the solutions women have come up with over the years has worked. Here's just a sampling of what parenting experts suggest working mothers do to create balance: don't bring your work home with you, even the mental part; have weekly pow-wow sessions with your family to coordinate the week's activities; spend all day Sunday making dinners for the week; set three daily priorities; establish your goals; make time to plan; don't cram on the weekends; or take some time for yourself when you come home before you put on your Mom hat. These women try hard to implement these strategies, but all they succeed in doing is using up even more time trying to make life work.

Nevertheless, we continue to look for that magical answer—for we'd rather bear the stress of trying to balance it all than admit it isn't possible. "Women who juggle for a living and do it badly—which is to say, most of us—spend so much time chasing dropped balls that they have little energy to observe, let alone to question, the rules of the game," writes Maushart.[9]

Even an article in *Working Mother* concedes that when mothers attempt to balance work and family, it's more likely work will intrude on their home lives rather than the other way around. The article refers to a report that was done by the Families and Work Institute: "A demanding job leaves almost half of parents too tired to do things with their children; 60% of working mothers say they have to put work ahead of family at least some of the time; overworked employees feel less successful in relationships with spouses, children, and friends; and they're more likely to lose sleep and feel stress."[10]

Nevertheless, working mothers persevere. And in their search for balance, they may turn to women like Katherine Wyse Goldman, author of *Working Mothers 101: How to Organize Your Life, Your Children, and Your Career to Stop Feeling Guilty and Start Enjoying It All*, who makes a valiant attempt to help women 'have it all.' But her book does nothing of the sort. What it does do, remarkably well actually, is teach women how to do the bare minimum when it comes to raising children. Goldman also overlooks the many ironies in her own book. She begins by observing that "No mother has ever regretted on her deathbed that she didn't spend enough time at the office" but spends the rest of the book telling women how they can organize their lives and farm out their family responsibilities so they *can* spend the majority of their time at the office.

She admits that dropping one's children off at daycare and picking them up isn't hard. What's hard, she says, is "that other part of being a mother: turning your innocent, guileless, perfect baby into an adult who's caring, compassionate, sensible, and responsible."[11] This last part is precisely what being an at-home mother is about. But if you're not home to do this work, then turning one's baby into a "caring, sensitive, compassionate, sensible, and responsible adult" will be difficult, if not impossible.

Goldman goes on to admit that she and other working mothers "have to rely a lot on others to know what is going on" with their children and that they "feel terribly guilty that we're not around all the time to guide our children through the minefield of life."[12] She adds, "We work hard, we work late, and we're distracted. As much as we want to think of nothing but our children when we're home, thoughts of impending deadlines creep into our thoughts."[13] Her solution is never the obvious one—to quit your job for the time being or at least cut back your hours. She tells women instead to capture quality moments with their children. Take a few moments to lie down with them at night before they go to sleep, she says. Noting daycare workers say children of working mothers always seem tired (I discuss this in the next chapter), she responds, "Big deal."[14]

Women are so dedicated to the feminist cause that women can bring home the bacon and fry it up in a pan, they refuse to accept this lifestyle causes a ripple effect, as each part of life spills over into the next and creates disaster. We just can't see that trying to perform two full-time jobs results in a time deficit and that no amount of organization is going to change this fact. "Time-use surveys confirm that as women enter the workplace, they take on the equivalent of two full-time jobs, forcing them to cut back on everything in their lives but paid work and children," writes Ann Crittenden.[15] And yet it's this other part of our lives—these things we're cutting back on—that allow us to lead happy, healthy lives.

Perhaps the greatest fallout of the two-income lifestyle is what happens to parents' evenings and weekends, coveted time that used to be reserved for spouses, children and oneself. These hours are now filled with an endless array of errands and household chores. Feminists gripe that the reason for this is women are expected to do the lion's share of housework and childcare. As Betty Freidan writes in the re-released *The Feminine Mystique*, "As we approach a new century—and a new millennium—it's the men who have to break through to a new way of thinking about themselves and society."[16] She says this despite admitting several pages earlier that American men "are now doing 40% of the housework and child care."[17] But that's not good enough, she writes. "Men are not yet taking absolutely equal responsibility for children and home."[18]

Here's the skinny about the so-called 50/50 marriage. Unless you've married a Neanderthal, equality has very little to do with what happens to the nights and weekends in a dual-income family. The reason for the ripple effect is time. "The battles [between husbands and wives] aren't always waged over actual chores or the inequity of handling them. The battle is over time," writes Rhonda Nordin in *After the Baby*.[19]

If two people are trying to raise children, bring home a paycheck, take out the trash, pay the bills, mow the lawn, paint the shutters, fix the leaky faucet, cook the meals, clean the dishes, go to Target, do the laundry, pick up the dry cleaning, go to Home Depot, shop for clothes, go to the doctor, return phone calls, do the grocery shopping, go to the gym, and drive their older kids all over God's creation, they're going to be in overload. No matter how well parents plan this time, no matter who's supposed to be in charge of what, it rarely runs smoothly. And one person always ends up doing more than the other.

This stress couples face is yet another fallout of the two-income family. There's simply no question that parents who both work full-time outside the home run in to far more conflict than they would if one of the parents wasn't employed. Take, for example, when one of their children gets sick. Who will take off work to stay home with them? This often becomes a major bone of contention.

As do household chores. When both parents work, there's usually not a default parent in charge of specific things at home— say, cooking for the family. When one parent stays home, it's logical for that person to be in charge of household matters; but when both parents are employed, all the work that needs to get done at home with respect to household maintenance and childcare is up for grabs. And that scenario, as we've seen in this book, creates a breeding ground for conflict.

It's also important to distinguish between a job and a career. A job that you can walk away from after 5 o'clock is very different from a career. The pressures on any person who pursues a demanding career are great, and that's what makes trying to take on the myriad of responsibilities at home simultaneously so difficult. When two people in a marriage are doing this, the opportunity for conflict escalates. All too often, the money from a second income isn't worth the turmoil it creates in the family's lifestyle.

The Nature of Guilt and Stress

All conversations about mothers at work eventually land in the same place: guilt. If you throw yourself into all the literature written by working mothers about their lives (although I wouldn't recommend it), you will find yourself overwhelmed with conversations about guilt. This group is forever trying to find a way to avoid their guilt, justify their guilt or blame their guilt on others. Facing their guilt head on, understanding why it's there in the first place, is never brought up, let alone entertained.

Guilt used to be a relatively simple concept. If you did something wrong, you knew it. Your conscience would tug at you, and you would feel bad. And you would continue to feel bad until you rectified the situation. When it comes to motherhood, however, guilt is a bit more complicated. There are two kinds of guilt mothers feel. There's real guilt, the kind that eats away at you because you know you've done something wrong and your conscience is not letting you off the hook; and there's unfounded guilt, the kind that rears its ugly head at a mother's slightest misstep but is, for the most part, fleeting and irrational.

Maria Shriver acknowledges these two aspects of guilt in her book, *Ten Things*. She defines guilt as her "gut talking to me."[20] She says that as a working mother she felt guilty all the time and was concerned that her children might think Boris Yeltsin was more important to her than they were. Now that she's a full-time mom, she says her children joke with her by telling her she's not around enough. "But the difference is," she says, "I let it roll off my back, because I know it's not true. If it were true, the guilt would be intolerable."[21]

Mothers desperately want to do right by their children. It is natural and normal to fear that any slip in one's mothering will cause our children irreparable harm. But we've distorted such insecurities by suggesting mothers shouldn't feel bad about not being present in their children's lives. And that's a whole different kind of guilt.

If I get a babysitter for a few hours so I can go house shopping or go out with my friends in the evening, or if my husband and I want to use a sitter on a Friday or Saturday night, I think nothing of it because I have the advantage of knowing my daughter has my care and attention for the majority of her waking hours. Now if I were away from my daughter all day, every day—*no matter what the reason*—you can bet I'd feel guilty. Because if I chose to be away from my daughter that much during the day, I wouldn't feel right about spending even more time away from her in the evenings. My conscience would always be there, tugging at me.

There's no way to feel serious, debilitating guilt if there is nothing to feel guilty about. A woman who cannot rid herself of guilt, whose heart feels as though it is being crushed, has simply made a bad decision. This is the nature of guilt, and it is the same guilt that all mothers feel when they choose to place their children in someone else's care.

Susan Chira argues that working mothers wouldn't feel guilty if they lived in a society that encouraged them to be proud of their choice to work outside the home: "One weekend morning, when I was too exhausted to even play with my children, I struggled to hold back tears, lashing myself with the same accusations that enraged me when others leveled them at working mothers."[22]

No mother would "lash herself" because of what others think about her lifestyle unless she herself feels ambivalent about it. Women who work to pay the rent or the mortgage—single moms, for example—would never find themselves in Chira's shoes, "lashing themselves," because they know they have no choice in the matter. They may feel a pang of guilt for not being around more, but they're never forced to wonder whether or not they're doing the right thing because they're not making a choice at all.

That's what I meant when I wrote earlier that this isn't a working class issue. It's a middle- and upper-middle class debate. The flipside of choice is responsibility. If we eschew it, we must deal with the consequences—one of which is guilt. As Judy Chicago, a former feminist, tells Smith College graduates, "If you choose to raise children, your careers will suffer; and if you choose careers, your kids will suffer—and so will you from the guilt and compromises you'll be forced to make."

This guilt working mothers feel is real, and nobody is doing it to them. Women are simply doing too much, and they know it. When they try to enjoy the simple pleasures in life—taking a long bath, going on a date with her husband, having a weekend afternoon to herself—they're hit with a wave of guilt. How can I get a babysitter and go out at night when my children haven't seen me all day? How can I steal a few hours to myself when my children never get to see me? And more often than not, she will give these things up—which ultimately leads to her frustration and discontent.

Nowhere is a mother's guilt more palpable than when she decides to place her baby in daycare. "It was really hard for me.

I cried. It took me two weeks to realize I wasn't harming him. I felt so guilty," writes Donna Perlowski, a Dallas mother, when she first took her son to daycare.[23] Perlowski is not alone. Most women are wracked with guilt when they first take their babies to daycare. I would be concerned about any parent who isn't wracked with guilt or anxiety upon dropping off a six-week old baby in the care of strangers all day, every day.

To be sure, the sensitivity of this subject makes it difficult to talk about. But as I said earlier, the goal isn't to make parents feel bad. The goal is to be honest, and we're not doing that. Rather than suggest mothers listen to their gut, the culture suggests daycare is both natural and normal. Over and over again, women are told that the guilt they feel has nothing to do with their consciences trying to tell the something. Rather, society has imposed this guilt upon them. So back to work Mom goes.

And the next time her conscience begins to nudge her, or the next time she sees something in her child that she believes may have to do with her absence, she reminds herself that these feelings have nothing to do with her. It's society's fault that she feels the way she does. Writers like Goldman assure her the guilty phase will pass. "Welcome to the top of the guilt list. You could spend months and years feeling terrible about leaving a tiny, adorable infant who has yet to sit up, much less take a step or say 'Mama,' but a better tactic is to dry your tears and suck it up."[24]

Suck it up.

So women give it a valiant effort. They leave the daycare center and head to the office to try to focus on work. Before long they're consumed with thoughts of their babies. They miss them; they worry about them; and in the back of their minds there's a gnawing sense of guilt. They find themselves unable to concentrate. But, again, no worry: "When you're at work, be there to contribute. When you're tempted to pick up the phone to check on the baby, you learn what guilt is all about. Train yourself to turn it off," writes Goldman.[25]

Train yourself to turn it off.

So women try again. And several months or years later, they begin to overcompensate for their absence from home. Some pull out all the stops for their children's birthday parties, thinking an elaborate event will somehow make their children forgive them for being gone so much. Or they buy their children gifts for no particular reason. And just when they think they've suppressed the guilt, it resurfaces in some other way.

This group of mothers finds themselves in a constant battle with their consciences that's evident each time they talk about their lives. Have a conversation with the average working mom, and you'll soon discover much of it is devoted to her explanation for *why* she has chosen to work outside the home. That feeling of angst is always there.

Stress is another big problem in dual-income families. The media love to talk about stress as though it were an everyday thing for most Americans. They routinely seek "experts" who make suggestions as to how parents can relieve their stress. Sue Shellenbarger's article in *Parade* magazine, which discussed the balancing act of a typical two-income family, was refreshingly candid: "The couple rose at 5:00 AM, rushed through breakfast, raced to drop their daughter at daycare, commuted thirty miles in opposite directions to demanding jobs, and raced back to pick up Muriel."[26]

Mary, the mother, tells Shellenbarger that she and her husband didn't have time for each other and that whatever time they did have was spent on household chores. She said that the strain was affecting their marriage and that their daughter was showing signs of anxiety. "The way we were living had to change," says Mary.[27] When they realized their priorities had "gone awry,"[28] the answer seemed obvious: Richard, the father, quit his job.

While such stories aren't rare, we rarely hear about them. It almost seems as though being stressed has become a desirable trait. For as much as we complain, having too much on our plates makes us feel important. Philipson writes about an occasion in which she and her co-workers were trying to find a mutually desirable time to meet once a month. As they perused their date books to look for possible dates, they realized they could not find a time to meet. Philipson noticed, much to her dismay, that everyone in the group "seemed proud of their overburdened schedules. Suddenly we seemed to be engaged in one-upmanship."[29]

Women's endless search for balance has all been for naught. More important, it has come at the expense of children and families. *There is no way to do everything at once.* We are not more fulfilled as a result of this lifestyle—we are less fulfilled. The only way families can end the madness is if one parent quits working or at least cuts back. If they do, they'll find a whole new life awaits them.

* * *

It is time, not money, Americans need. The more time we have, the better our quality of life. As Orenstein writes about one of the working mothers she interviewed for her book, "Time has been the biggest trade-off in the balance [Emily] has struck between family life and work. Time alone, time with Dan, time with friends, and particularly, time with the children."[30] Amy, working mother of two, tells Familyeducation.com, "I'm either working or with my kids. I've decided not to do things for myself, like work out, read a book, or spend time with my friends. There's no 'me time.' You're 'on' at the office, you're 'on' at home. I know intellectually I need to create that balance, but it never happens."[31]

As a mom and a writer, I too can relate. Despite being in a highly desirable situation—I work for myself, from home, and mostly during "off hours"—even I can't escape the fallout. In my case, there were three areas I didn't compromise in my choice to write this book. The first was my daughter; the second was sleep; and the third was exercise.

I told myself that as long as I made these three areas my top priority, I could handle other areas of my life taking a back seat for a while. The areas I neglected were household chores, leisure time, and my marriage. The moment my daughter went down for her nap (which lasted about two and a half hours) and the moment she went down for the night (about 7:30 PM), I went to work. I did not watch television; I did not read for pleasure; I did not clean the house; I did not answer the phone; and I prepared the simplest meals I could. I did manage to go out every so often on Friday and Saturday nights, which was a good thing because those were the times my husband and I were able to spend time together.

Suffice it to say, I was thrilled to have finished the book. After all, what's the point of being married if you never spend any time with your spouse? What's the point of having a kitchen if you're never going to cook? What's the point of owning a home if you're not going to take care of it? What's the point of having friends if you never talk to them? (What's the point of having children if you're not going to raise them?)

The problem is that time is an intangible, so we tend to dismiss it. We prefer to think of time as an hour here, an hour there, but rarely do we consider the emotional spillover that takes place. "Even if there's physical time for friends, family, community, and personal reflection, there's no psychic space left," writes Robert Reich.[31]

Many women insist the answer to this problem is organization, or the ability to carve out family time. Goldman suggests "don't make plans with other couples on Saturday night. Stay home and make dinner with the family."[32] (There go your friendships.) Or "try to have dinner as a family, even if the children have to wait for you to get home."[33] (Now your kids are cranky because they're hungry.) Or "make plans for one day each weekend."[34] (How will the errands and chores get done?) These suggestions merely result in stealing time away from other things.

As Arlie Hochschild observes, "Paradoxically, what may seem to harried working parents like a solution to their time bind—efficiency and time segmentation—can later feel like a problem in itself."[35] Indeed, moving faster in order to create quality time does not result in quality time at all because quality time ends up taking a "special discipline, focus, and energy, just like work."[35] Parents also discover that wrench after wrench is thrown into their plans because they didn't anticipate the general spontaneity of life: the things they didn't plan for but which nevertheless came up.

We don't get it. *There is no time.* The only way to find time is for someone to quit working so much and spend more time at home. The less we do, the more time we have. The more time we have, the more connected we feel. The more connected we feel, the happier we are.

Less is more.

"But," say feminists, "if society would support us, we *could* get it all done!" Peggy Orenstein asserts that "maybe it's not mothers' withdrawal from the workplace that's called for but support, appreciation, and reassurance—from employers, friends, family, and in particular, husbands."[36] But employers, friends, family, and husbands have been nothing but supportive. Indeed, there has never been a better time in history for mothers to be supported in their choice to work outside the home. Most companies are as family-friendly as they possibly can be. Even *Working Mother* admits it's "unrealistic to expect any company to meet all its employees' child-care needs."[37]

And not only are today's husbands more involved at home, they fully support their wives' choice to work, whether they want this lifestyle or not. When was the last time you heard a man say he'd prefer it if his wife would stay home? He'd rather stick needles in his eyes! The reason work-family balance continues to be elusive is not the insensitivity of men and employers but because raising children has always been, and will continue to be, a full-time job. And no one, male or female, can successfully perform two full-time jobs at the same time.

This has been true since women first attempted the juggling act. In the 1960s, my mother tried to combine a career as a stockbroker with motherhood. Despite having an ideal setup, a nanny-housekeeper and a job two minutes from home, her balancing act lasted less than five years. She thought it was working well when she had one child, but after I came along everything changed. There was simply no time, energy or ability to do it all.

Balance was still elusive in 1989, when Hochschild interviewed Ann Myerson, working mother of two, for Hochschild's book *The Second Shift*. Myerson told Hochschild that she tried all the strategies to create balance: she kept her children up at night to spend "quality time" with them; she farmed out most of her household duties to her children's nanny; she left her work, physically and mentally, at the office; and she cut back on spending time with friends. But nothing worked. "I don't like what's going on at home. My husband is terrific. I've had all the help money could buy. I've had a fifteen-minute commute, and it still hasn't worked out."[38] So she quit.

Fourteen years later, here's how another woman describes her former life as a working mother to Nordin and Gjerdingen: "I got the baby ready for daycare, dropped her off, and picked her up each day after work. Then I fixed dinner, cleaned up the kitchen, bathed the baby, put her to bed, and with whatever energy I had left, picked up the debris left around the rest of the house. On weekends, I ran errands, picked up groceries, really cleaned the house, did laundry—and, oh yes, spent "quality time" with the baby. I lost all track of family and friends, dropped all volunteer activities, and gained 10 lbs. Bedtime became my opiate. And, of course, I didn't feel like making love. I was exhausted."[39]

The beauty of staying home, if only for a few years, is that it offers women enormous flexibility. One of the best things about it is that mothers never need to rush. Whatever they can't accomplish one day, they can always accomplish the next. There are no deadlines to be met, and there's no one to answer to.

That alone is worth giving up a paycheck.

CHAPTER 5

RAISING KIDS IN A RUSH

Children flourish when they are unhurried.

— *Inda Schaenen*

If you've ever walked alongside a child—or bathed, dressed or fed a child—you know how slow children are. It begins at birth and continues all the way through adolescence, as parents anxiously tap their feet waiting for teenagers to gather their belongings for school. Children, by their very nature, move like snails. We, unfortunately, do not. Ever since work became our priority and technology accelerated our lives, we've been busy, active, on the go. I guess we thought children would adjust.

We thought wrong.

Society may change, but children don't. Each of their activities—walking, dressing, eating, bathing, playing, talking, learning—is excruciatingly slow. Previous generations had an easier time adapting to this reality, for an obvious reason: life was slower. Today we expect children to adapt to our pace. If things don't move quickly enough for us, we can't be bothered. Our accelerated lifestyle controls us, so much we don't even think we have a choice to slow down. We really believe that.

So we've come up with a new way to raise children. We begin by removing babies from their cribs while they're still asleep so we can get them to daycare in time for work. We shuffle older children around from home to school to activity as though they're in our way, and we need a place to put them. We no longer feed children three healthy meals a day because it takes us too much time to prepare, and it takes children too long to eat. Finally, we no longer talk to our children, really talk, because we're just too tired to give them our full attention.

And still we wrinkle our eyebrows and wonder what's wrong with children today. Why are they not doing well in school? Why are they overweight? Why are they getting into so much trouble? Why are they sleep deprived? Why are they on Ritalin? Why are they disrespectful? Why are they spoiled? We simply refuse to see the connection between the problems that exist among today's children and the fact that mothers aren't home. Just what did we think mothers were for?

I remember combing through an issue of *Parenting* magazine and stumbling upon the "Work and Family" section. There it was in bold print: a suggestion for how working mothers could fit their children into their lives. It read, "When you get home, set a timer for 15 minutes, then curl up with your child to read a book together or just listen to the tales about her day. By the time the buzzer goes off, she'll have had enough of a mom fix that you can start preparing supper."[1]

Welcome to motherhood in the twenty-first century.

Americans have come to believe it's the quality, not quantity, of time we spend with our children that matters. We've talked ourselves into believing we can raise children with leftover time, as if a relationship with a child can be built within a certain number of hours we've set aside to make it happen. But it doesn't work that way. "Being a good parent isn't about measured minutes. It's about relationships, especially the primary love relationship we call 'attachment,'" writes Penelope Leach in *Child* magazine.[2] When mothers do not take the time and put forth the effort required to establish a healthy, working relationship with their children, they will not enjoy the benefits that come from this work.

That's one of the reasons some parents find themselves in power struggles with their young children. Jane Sullivan, working mother of two, tells *Newsweek* that her son purposely takes an hour to do homework that shouldn't take more than twenty minutes. "He doesn't see us much, and this is time to act out," says Sullivan, adding, "We have battles in which he tests us. Maybe this is his way of getting us to fully focus on him."[3] Sullivan is not alone. That is the result when parents make children a sideline occupation.

The number of hours parents spend with their children absolutely, unequivocally matters. Children aren't supposed to fit into our lives—we're supposed to fit into theirs. What children need is the undivided attention and loyalty of one adult, preferably their mothers. Anything less isn't good enough.

Women who know this best are at-home mothers who were once working mothers. This is an ever-growing group that's been largely overlooked. Jane, a former teacher, compared her current experience with motherhood to that when she was working full-time. "I know firsthand what a difference time makes with kids. My five-year-old daughter had spent an enormous amount of time on a project for school that she needed my help with and was extremely enthused about it. I know her creation would not have produced the same results had I been "working" because the attention span of a kindergartner would not have allowed her to cram everything into a couple of evenings or a weekend.

More importantly, I was there for encouragement and praise along the way. I could say that I would have done this a year ago, but honestly, I would have been trying to accomplish multiple tasks as she was working on it, and depending on the day and my work demands, my entire demeanor would not have been the same. The completion of the task would have carried far more weight than the actual process, going totally against what I tried to teach my own students for so many years. So in the end, it was my time and undivided attention that made the difference."[4]

Another former working mom tells me she remembers "all too well the dreaded morning routine when I was working full-time: a run at 4:45 AM, a 5-minute shower, a 'breakfast' consumed at an unhealthy speed, and then rushing upstairs to push and prod my oldest son along to get dressed and downstairs to eat so I could begin the 7:15 morning commute to work."[5] She adds, "Soon after I quit my job, my son said to me one morning as I was brushing his hair, 'We don't have to hurry, hurry, hurry anymore, Mom.'" Let's face it: parents don't have the energy to give kids what they need if their energy and drive has been depleted by a day at the office.

As former working mother Jean Blockhus-Grover says, "Despite my strength with organization, a high degree of energy, and having a husband who is great with doing his part, I often felt as if my head was barely above water." Sarah Bridges, a licensed psychologist who quit her job to stay home with her children, remembers her life as a working mom: "I didn't like how my kids became items on my to-do list. I hurried through our evenings, dying for the minute they would all go to sleep."[6]

Not long ago I ran into a woman I used to know who's now a working mother, and we spent a good part of the evening discussing her life as a mom. Here's what Sarah's life looks like: She rises each day at 4:30 AM, wakes her three and a half-year-old daughter up sometime before 6:00 AM, and begins her forty-minute commute to work. (Breakfast is eaten in the car.) On the way, she and her husband drop their daughter off at daycare and pick her up nine or ten hours later to head back home for some "quality time." In order to make room for this, the daughter stays up until 9:00 PM.

As the night wore on, Sarah rationalized her life this way: she "loves her daughter's daycare"; she's "a better mom for working"; she "spends a lot of quality time with her daughter" (though she would later reveal that, invariably, "all hell breaks loose" after work, making quality time elusive). And through it all, it was obvious she was conflicted. She even mentioned that if she and her husband have another child, her husband would have to stay home. (I presume she said it would be her husband because she makes more money, but I certainly didn't ask.)

Twice in the evening our conversation was interrupted when her babysitter called to ask her to come home, which was only two houses away. It seems her daughter wouldn't go to sleep without seeing her. (It was, after all, a Friday night; and her daughter hadn't seen her mother all day.) At 11:00 PM, Sarah left for the last time. But she called me at the party to tell me something she hadn't finished telling me earlier because she knew I wanted to share her story in my book. She said every week her daughter asks her, "Is it the weekend yet, Mommy?" And on one particular week Sarah asked her daughter what she wanted to do over the weekend. Her daughter replied, "Play in my playroom, stay together and have a family."

I remember being torn that night. I was struck by Sarah's honesty, since it was obvious she was not happy with her current arrangement. At one point her eyes began to well up with tears, and it felt as though she were searching for an answer. And because she was not a stranger to me, I desperately wanted to say something helpful. But I knew the only answer I could offer would be the one she wouldn't want to hear. So I said nothing.

What I wanted to say was that her daughter needs her. What I wanted to say was that the reason her three-and-a-half-year old was still awake at 11:00 p.m. was that she's starving for her mother's attention. What I wanted to say was, although she may consider herself "a better mom for working," her daughter doesn't see it that way. What I wanted to tell her was that that there's plenty of research that concludes what children want most from their parents is for them to "be there," not just physically but mentally. "In my conversations with them, children from kindergarten to age twelve overwhelmingly indicate that what they want most is more time, as in undivided attention," writes Dr. Ron Taffel, a family therapist and author of *The Second Family*."[7] He adds, "The quality of family life has changed dramatically."[7]

Indeed it has. Gone are the days when babies and toddlers were home with their mothers, when morning meant moving slowly, when children played in their neighborhoods and were called inside at dusk, when TV viewing was limited, when homework was supervised, when bedtime was early, and when illness and obesity was rare. That childhood has been replaced with daycare, after-school care, fast food, unlimited screen time, latchkey kids, countless extra-curricular activities, no downtime, sleep deprivation, and childhood obesity.

The most powerful voices in America would like us to believe it's a coincidence the well being of our nation's children has declined at the same time there's been a surge of mothers entering the workforce. It is no coincidence. The most powerful voices in America also claim there are many ways to be a good mother, that being at home is only one option. It is true there are many ways to be a good mother. But women cannot be good at something, or even bad at something, if they're not present in the first place.

Mothering is harder and more important than any other job in the world—most people have no trouble acknowledging this fact. But saying it and believing it are two different things. The truth is, our culture does not view raising children as work at all, as evident by the common refrain that parents whose children sleep, eat, and behave well are simply "lucky."

A mother is "lucky" if her child takes a nap or goes to sleep at night without a fuss; a mother is "lucky" if her child eats fruits and vegetables; a mother is "lucky" if her child behaves well. It is simply easier to believe children become who they become by sheer luck. If we believe this, it means we can avoid the hard work altogether. It means when both parents work outside the home, it's okay—because who our children become has nothing to do with the way they're raised. They come out the way they come out.

That's a convenient idea; but healthy, well-rested and well-behaved children are the tangible result of a mother's hard work. I am *not* suggesting, and this is very important, that all children of stay-at-home mothers are healthy and well behaved. What I'm saying is that it takes, at minimum, a parent's physical and emotional presence to be able to make it happen at all. In other words, the mere presence of a mother doesn't ensure a good outcome, but her lack of presence usually does.

It's just unreasonable to suggest there's no difference between a woman who stays at home to do the work of motherhood and one who doesn't. The only folks who believe this are those who do not understand the needs of children. So for the purpose of clarification, let's take a look at some of what those needs are.

Children's Health

While the media is quick to report statistics about sleep deprivation and childhood obesity, what they rarely report is the connection between these problems and the absence of mothers from home. Journalists frequently furrow their brows and ask experts why such things are happening to today's children. And the response is always the same: children are far too sedentary.

They do not get enough exercise; they eat too much junk food; and they spend far too much time in front of the television.

What the experts never say is why. Because that one small detail—mothers aren't around to keep their children on track—is too much truth to swallow. It is the most off-limits topic in history. That's why when parents ask pediatricians or other experts why their children aren't sleeping, eating or behaving well, most receive the stereotypical politically correct response: "Some children need more sleep than others," or "Johnny's metabolism is a little off," or "Johnny is going through an aggressive phase."

On the surface, such responses may seem harmless. They certainly do a lot to assuage parental guilt. But what the experts will not say, what they can't say, is that children do not learn these things on their own. If Mom or Dad isn't there to teach them, it's not going to happen.

Sleep

Sleep has been one of the first things parents have compromised in their desire to live a fast-paced life. And that's fine—for them. But parents assume children's sleep can be compromised as well, and it can't. Not without a huge cost to them and the family as a whole. "A good night's sleep, much like nutrition, seat belts, and a roof over one's head, is an inalienable right of every child and a bona fide parental responsibility," writes Dr. Judith Owens, director of the Pediatric Sleep Disorders Clinic at Brown University School of Medicine.[8]

Indeed, any pediatrician or sleep expert can tell you that children need a lot of sleep. Sleep is as necessary to their physical and emotional health as food and exercise. The difference between a child who has had enough sleep and one who hasn't cannot be overstated. A child who is well rested is joyful, content, and happy. A child who is sleep deprived—or just plain tired—is antsy, difficult, and, as Inda Schanen writes in *The 7 O'Clock Bedtime*, "wears his fatigue like a suit of itchy, ill-fitting clothing."[9]

There is a direct correlation between sleep and behavior. "Kids' behavior is a telltale sign of whether or not they're getting enough sleep," writes Dr. Marc Weissbluth, author of *Healthy Sleep Habits, Happy Child*.[10] Unfortunately, many do not see the connection between their children's poor sleep habits and their erratic behavior. "If a child has poor sleep habits, his parents will think that he just doesn't need a lot of sleep. That's probably not true—in fact, it's likely that such a child is actually sleep-deprived," says Dr. Jodi Mindell, sleep expert for Baby Center. com.[11]

Although the amount of sleep children need varies somewhat, most experts agree on the following estimates:

Infants: About 16 hours (2 naps)
One-year-old: About 14 hours (1 nap)
Ages 2-4: About 13 hours (1 nap)
Ages 5-11: About 11 hours
Ages 12-18: About 9 hours

In the desire to live fast-paced lives, some mothers cut corners on their children's naps—or even stop their naps long before they should. As Diane Fisher observes, "It is unfortunate that our society is impatient with slow, subtle infant schedules in their fast, goal-oriented culture."[12] At-home mothers, whether they're successful in this area or not, are at least in a position to try and make it happen. Working mothers are not. They are at the mercy of their children's caregivers and are thus unable to control or even monitor their children's sleep habits. That's why their children are notoriously sleep deprived.

In most dual-income families, children are awakened before their bodies wake naturally and rushed out the door before they're even awake. These parents also aren't around during the day to make sure their children sleep during the day. They also keep their children up at night long after they should because they haven't seen them all day. Add it all up, and the result is obvious: sleep deprivation.

There's no way to ensure children get what they need if there's no parent around to see that it happens. If parents want their children to get the sleep they need, and if they want them to take a nap and go to sleep at night without a big production, they need to develop a routine early on—say, when their children are around four months old—and stick with it. All babies do not need to be on the same schedule, but they do need the same schedule every day. You can't do one thing one day and another thing the next and expect your baby to sleep the way you want him to. Children will only be compliant if they know what to expect.

Children also need good quality naps, say Weissbluth and Mindell. This means they should not be napping in cars and strollers (beyond the newborn stage), and their naps should be at the same time every day in a quiet room with little or no noise in order to get optimal sleep. "Catching" naps here and there will not produce the desired outcome. "Studies in adults have shown that irregular sleep-wake patterns lead to significant alterations in our moods and sense of well-being, and undermine our ability to sleep at the desired times. The same is true of young children, although many parents don't seem to appreciate this fact," writes Richard Ferber in *Solve Your Child's Sleep Problems.*[13]

So how can you tell if your child is sleep deprived? If you find yourself waking your child up on a regular basis, or if your child falls asleep in the car on a regular basis or wakes up frequently in the middle of the night, your child is most likely overtired. If he seems cranky or irritable during the day or if he falls asleep much earlier than his usual bedtime, this is also a good sign he's sleep deprived.

Weissbluth also points out that most kids who don't sleep well are going to bed too late. He notes that many parents make the mistake of thinking if they keep their children up at night or let them skip a nap they'll become so tired that they'll just fall into bed at night—the way an adult might. But it doesn't work that way. "The better rested kids are, the easier it is for them to fall asleep, and the easier it is for them to stay asleep longer."[14]

Food

Perhaps the most significant fallout of the two-income family is children's eating habits. Nutrition is as critical to a child's emotional and physical development as sleep. "Like sleep, food is not optional in life, but its quality is," writes Inda Schaenan.[15] Unfortunately, many parents cut corners because they lack the time to tend to this part of life.

For these families, dinnertime can be as elusive as breakfast; and many parents resort to convenience foods. "Working parents arrive home long after the stomachs of children demand to be filled," writes Reich.[16] Lucky for them, they have plenty of support for doing so. Virtually every food commercial or advertisement makes sure to add that such-and-such food can be prepared in fifteen minutes or less. Moreover, supermarkets now offer meals in which all the work has already been done. All parents need to do is know how to operate a microwave.

Easier, that is, until her conscience gets the better of her and she realizes she should probably spend some time in the kitchen if she wants her children to be healthy. But, of course, she can't. She doesn't have time. "Cutting, chopping, dragging out the pans, sautéing, boiling, and broiling are not pleasures during the week. Besides, you have to change your clothes so you don't get the suit messed up—but if you're late getting home, then you don't have time to change, and if you're eating fast to run to parents' night at school, then you barely have time to eat anyway," writes Goldman.[17] Goldman's suggestion for working mothers? "Don't get bent out of shape when your kid won't eat the dinner. You don't have that much emotion invested in it in the first place. Point to the options: the boxes of cereal."[18]

It is this kind of thinking that caused our children's health to decline. Indeed, researchers at Pennsylvania State University studied the eating habits of seven-year-old girls and their mothers and found the fussy eaters tended to be children whose "mothers didn't have much time to help their kids eat healthy, so instead of trying to feed them a wide variety of foods, the moms would offer foods they knew their children would eat."[19] Naturally, such foods are often high in salt, sugar, and fat.

Teaching children how to eat is an enormous task. If you want to do it right, you have to spend several hours a day in the kitchen. I know it's tedious to sit down with a toddler or young child three times a day and make sure the fruits and vegetables get from the plate to the mouth when all children really want is dessert. But if we don't do it, they suffer. And so do we when we cannot get them to eat well down the road.

As Leann Birch, a psychologist at Penn State University, writes, "Most children reject things at first. It takes multiple exposures—sometimes as many as ten times—before kids come to accept and like new foods they initially turned down."[20] This is one of the things that make parenting such a challenge, but avoiding the challenge has hurt us deeply. "According to the latest federal figures, the percentage of youngsters ages 6-11 who are overweight has tripled since the 1960s," writes Shannon Brownlee on Time.com.[21]

The percentage of overweight children has tripled since the 1960s. (Wasn't that when mothers began to leave their homes in search of greener pastures?) Brownlee adds that the Surgeon General "issued an urgent call for the nation to fight its growing weight problem"[22] and discusses the even more alarming number of children with diabetes. Brownlee's suggestion for parents is to not let their kids get into the habit of eating high-fat, high-sugar foods and out of the habit of getting regular exercise. Well, yes, this is obvious. But the only way this can occur is if a parent is home to see that it happens. Naturally, the article neglects to mention that part.

So how can mothers make sure children eat well, maintain a balanced diet and avoid overeating? First, by accepting that it takes an enormous amount of time and energy to do it right and then put forth that effort. Anyone who can read can cook. It isn't rocket science—it's just a helluva lot of work.

Second, start your baby off on the right track. As soon as he begins eating solid foods, introduce healthy foods. "It is very easy to introduce new foods to kids between about 9 and 18 months, when they are putting anything in their mouth,"[23] says Dr. Susan B. Roberts, professor of nutrition and psychiatry at Tufts University. If a baby has never had anything sugary, he will not have anything to compare the "good" foods with, so even if he doesn't take to the healthy foods right away, he probably will eventually. "Kids are born with a sweet tooth, but they have to learn to enjoy other tastes," says Birch.[24]

Third, eat well yourself. Babies and toddlers will do exactly as their parents do—they have no choice! "Everyone grows up with food preferences that are largely programmed by the foods around them," says Roberts. "So what you put on your table, and what children see their parents eating and enjoying, has a big influence."[25]

Here's a great example. I introduced my daughter to Shredded Wheat (plain, no sugar) early on when I couldn't get her to eat oatmeal. She took to it because it was something different, and I think this alone made it appealing. Several months down the road, however, I bought Honeycomb because I love Honeycomb. My plan was not to let my daughter see the box, not because I'm a health nut or because I think it would be harmful for her to eat it, but because I knew that as long as Honeycomb was an option she would choose it over the Shredded Wheat. But I relented in a weak moment and gave her a few pieces to snack on. Big mistake. As long as she saw that box of Honeycomb on top of the refrigerator, that was all she wanted. So much for the Shredded Wheat.

Fourth, and this is by far the most important: *feed your children when they're hungry*. That means not letting them snack a lot during the day. This is hard to do since snacks keeps babies and toddlers happy and content; but the hungrier young children are at mealtime, the more likely they are to eat whatever you put in front of them. Really! (And for the record, I use small bags of Cheerios or raisins as snacks. Oh, and Dum Dum lollipops.)

Discipline

Discipline is the hardest and most significant part of being a parent. Unfortunately, the tough love approach parents used to take has been replaced with the feel-good approach begun by Baby Boomers. It was this generation that began an era of parenting in which Mom and Dad became their children's friends. "Something happened to parenting as the job shifted from the World War II generation to its children, the baby boomers," writes Washington writer Leonard Pitts Jr. "Where previous generations were restrictive, baby boomers were permissive. Where previous generations gave orders, baby boomers negotiated. Mothers and fathers had been parents. Baby boomers became co-equals, playmates. And we're seeing the fruit of that approach. We're seeing kids who are disconnected, disaffected, materialistic, filled with a misplaced sense of entitlement and sometimes, just flat-out spoiled."[26]

There are four basic strategies for disciplining children. Be calm when giving orders, know when to ignore certain behaviors, reward good behavior, and be consistent in everything you do and say. Too many people think of discipline as being about punishment, but it isn't really. "Discipline is only in small part about punishment; in large part, it is about building character, testing self-esteem, and teaching social skills that will ultimately create a self-disciplined adolescent and adult," writes best-selling author Michael Gurian.[27]

Once parents accept this and stop being afraid of it, they can let go of the idea that discipline is a bad thing. "When discipline is seen as teaching and is conveyed with a great deal of empathy and nurturing care, children feel good when they comply. It is a warm, nourishing feeling to feel that you are the gleam in someone else's eye," writes Stanley Greenspan in *The Irreducible Needs of Children*.[28] When we discipline children responsibly, we prove to them how much we love them and care about their well being. When we continually negotiate or allow them to have their way, we tell them, in effect, that they are in charge of us.

I've seen this again and again in my teaching experience. Most kids who exhibit behavior problems are crying out for order. What seems like strictness to us is comfort for them. As Gurian puts it, "A child learns to be an authority by modeling after others who hold clear and competent authority. It is the child raised by people without strength who becomes weak. It is the child raised with high expectations who becomes independent."[29]

In other words, discipline begets discipline. Adults who have good self-discipline will have less trouble disciplining their children because it comes naturally to them. Just as unorganized, unscheduled or overweight parents tend to produce unorganized, unscheduled or overweight children, parents who do not eat, sleep (or even behave) well themselves struggle with their children when it comes to these matters.

There will always be parents who are better than others at discipline, just as there are teachers who are better at this than others. What's different today is that many mothers aren't home, which has two specific consequences. These parents are far more likely to experience power struggles with their children simply because they haven't been around on a consistent basis from day one. They've relied on others to do this work for them. This, in turn, causes their children to lash out, for they're confused about the boundaries. A mother has to earn the right to be obeyed, and this will only occur if she is present in her children's lives. If she makes this investment, she will reap the rewards. But if she has passed this work off to someone else, she will not.

The other problem is parents who are often absent are less inclined to discipline their children when they get home because they haven't seen them all day and don't want to spend what little time they do have fighting with their kids. "Working parents have a very tough time thinking about limits. Their ability to set limits has gone way down in this generation. Parents tell me, 'I can't stand to be away all day and then come back and be the disciplinarian,'" writes T. Berry Brazleton.[30] Greenspan notes that "parents don't feel that they have earned the right to set limits. If you feel that you are not there enough for your children, you might not feel right asking that child to be quiet while you talk to Dad about something important."[31]

Since the nights and weekends of two-income parents are consumed with chores and activities, and because they're exhausted from their workday, they can't muster the energy to discipline their children in a healthy, consistent fashion. Disciplining kids is a task that requires an enormous amount of patience. It is extremely difficult to muster such patience when you have the demands of the workplace pulling at you simultaneously. "It's easier to keep your temper when you don't have a train to catch," writes Gurdon.[32]

Overscheduling

Overscheduling is the term we came up with to describe the number of activities today's children are involved in. Many children now participate in so many activities they have no time to relax and play, which can and often does lead to poor mental health. Somewhere along the line, parents decided that packing in many organized activities will somehow make for smarter or more accomplished children. But it doesn't. All it does is put an emphasis on outward achievement and competition.

Too many people dismiss the necessity of good old-fashioned boredom. If children had the opportunity to be productive on their own, without having every moment filled in with unnecessary planned activities, parents would be amazed at how bright and creative their children could become. As Inda Schaenan puts it: "Yes, I do want my child to be bored. I want all my children to confront boredom, to come up against that blank wall of time and to have to find a way through that appeals to them as individuals. I do not want their lives so full and so fully planned that they never have to think about what to do next."[33]

But it isn't just the desire to have well-rounded children that leads parents to overschedule their kids. Working parents use these activities as a way of keeping their children occupied while they're at work. "Try as we might to suggest that all these enrichment activities are for the good of children, there is ample evidence that they are really for the convenience of parents with way too little leisure time of their own," writes Anna Quindlen.[34]

Helping our children organize their after-school lives and just being around is part of our job as parents. This is the time when children need someone to help them with their schoolwork, drive them to an extra-curricular activity and help cheer them on, talk through their problems, and answer questions. But, as Shaenan writes, "Some parents fill up their children's lives with classes and activities in order to avoid direct contact with their children, the kind of contact that is often grueling, frustrating, menial, laborious, and exhausting."[35]

Any good educator can tell you that parental involvement is critical to a child's success in school. It is rare to find a good student who doesn't have a strong parent in his court. As Susan Sherrod writes, "Studies have indicated that children whose parents and/or significant adults share in their formal education tend to do better in school," adding, "Children need and want their families to be involved in their lives."[36]

Consistency is the *controlling factor* in the health and well being of our children. More than anything, kids want and need to know they can count on us to do the same things tomorrow that we did today, and that we will ask the same things of them tomorrow that we did today. This is comforting to them, regardless of their age. "Consistency is the most important element in your relationship with your children, yet it is the most frequently omitted," writes Sal Severe in *How To Behave So Your Children Will Too.*[37]

Here's an example. My daughter and I have a routine at bedtime where I hold her "one more minute" and then put her down. Then I tell her I love her. And one night she said, "And Daddy loves you." (The "you" means her). And I would say, "Yes, and Daddy loves you." And so began our routine. Then one night when I kissed her and told her I loved her, I forgot to mention Daddy and proceeded to walk out of the room. She began to cry and in between sobs she was saying something, but I couldn't make it out. Then I finally heard her. She was screaming, "Daddy loves you, Daddy loves you!" So I had to go back into her room to assure that yes, "Daddy loves you, too." She immediately stopped crying and went to sleep.

Life after school

Americans have underestimated the significance of the hours children are not in school, that elusive yet critical time between 3:00 PM and bedtime during which a parent should be, well, parenting. We can attribute the surge of problems young people have today to what takes place during this time of day.

Some parents believe their job didn't actually begin until their children *started* school! A child's early years are all about eating and sleeping and diapers and toilet training and schedules and activities, but their later years are about eating and sleeping and schedules and activities and homework and school and transportation and clothes and friends. The needs of children change, but they do not diminish. As one former working mother says, "Babies' needs are pretty simple. But older kids require more: You've got to watch who they're bringing home; their homework gets more complex; and they have activities. It becomes more difficult to delegate that supervision to someone else."[38]

School-age children need a parent physically available when they're not at school. This is when the true parenting takes place, and it isn't happening. Millions of children fend for themselves. And with the exception of highly motivated teenagers, most end up in extended-day programs or go home to an empty house. And those who go home to an empty house—latchkey kids, we call them—are the most vulnerable to becoming overweight or depressed or to do poorly in school.

Out of concern for one of these problems, obesity, Oprah interviewed Melinda Southern, a pediatric physiologist and director for the Pediatric Obesity Clinical Research Section of the Louisiana State University Medical Center. Southern claimed that children are becoming heavier because of a decrease in physical activity made possible by modern transportation, television, computers, and video games, combined with the availability of high-caloric foods such as fast food, convenience foods and snacks. "Most children who become overweight and obese have a perfectly normal metabolism. The problem isn't their genes, but their environment," says Southern.[39]

Southern spoke with two of Oprah's guests, a mother and her overweight son. She asked them a series of questions about a typical day at their house and what the son did after school. The scenario went like this: Her son was alone after school or sometimes with his older sister or aunt. He watched television. The mother arrived home around dinnertime. When Southern tried to explain all the ways in which the mother could fix the problem with her son's weight, make sure he gets outside every day or is involved in some type of sporting activity, the mother explained that she couldn't be there to do those things because she works. Furthermore, she said, her son doesn't have any interest in being outside; he likes to do nothing. No matter what Southern suggested, the mother couldn't hear it. And the reason she couldn't is because the only way to help her son is to quit her job and come home.

For those who want to know what it is at-home mothers do, this is it. Children who eat, sleep, and behave well and who are successful in school are not accidents. Any parent who puts forth this same effort will reap the same rewards. As Woody Allen once said, "Eighty percent of success is showing up."[40]

CHAPTER 6

WHAT PARENTS NEED TO KNOW ABOUT NANNIES AND DAYCARE

You can't pay someone to do for a child what a parent will do for free. Even excellent childcare can never do what a good parent can do.

— *Urie Bronfenbrenner*

Married parents who work full-time and leave their children in substitute care are not bad parents. But most don't have backgrounds in child development, nor do they do research on the subject prior to hiring a nanny or putting their children in daycare. They should, though—particularly since the media won't touch the subject and parents are thus left in the dark when it comes to the needs of children. Parents don't realize they're allowing their power and influence to be substituted, and even undermined, by those with whom they leave their children. Because whomever a child spends the majority of his waking hours with is going to have an enormous impact on the person he later becomes.

Parents choose to put their faith in daycare because they're assured children don't really need their mothers. They'll be fine in daycare. "When we choose to put a child in daycare, we want to believe it's good, and so we do," writes Covey. He adds, "That which we desire most earnestly, we believe most easily."[1]

That which we desire most earnestly, we believe most easily.

The rationalizations run deep. Consider two of the women Susan Chira describes in *A Mother's Place*. One woman tells her, "My goal is to get home by 7:30 PM. My feeling is, if you miss bedtime, you blow it."[2] In this woman's misguided view of motherhood, she thinks it's fine to be absent from her children's lives as long as she wants *assuming* she shows up for bedtime. If she doesn't show up then, she's blown it.

Chira then introduces a friend of hers who she says has "responsibilities that often keep her at the office until 8:00 or 9:00 PM."[3] But no matter, says Chira, because "her half hour at her daughters' bedtime gives her a sense of intimacy and assurance that is evident every time I have seen her with her children."[4] Huh?

No reasonable person believes there's no difference between the type of "mothering" Chira and her friends think they do and the kind of mothering that takes place throughout the day, all week long. "Being fed and put to bed is a tiny fraction of what [children] need. Parents must provide time and energy to talk, play, read, and pay attention to their young children," writes Judith Wallerstein in *The Unexpected Legacy of Divorce*.[5]

Most Americans are in the dark about the bonding process that takes place in a child's first years of life. (Why wouldn't they be? They never hear about it!) The relationship between mother and child is delicate and time intensive, a byproduct of the day-in and day-out care that takes place. It is "not a quick bonding period—one that fits into today's typical twelve-week maternity leave. Rather, it is a slow, gradual process of many seemingly trivial communication cues and responses," writes Dr. Diane Fisher in her 1997 Congressional testimony regarding infant brain development.[6] When children have one adult they can depend on, when they hear the same voice talking to them and caring for them every day, they grow to feel worthy of love, secure in who they are and in what they are capable of becoming.

Even marginal care at home is better than daycare. Despite what feminists claim, an unfulfilled mother doesn't always translate to a bad mother. Unless the mother is causing her children physical or mental harm (which is not the norm), her children don't care whether or not she's happy. All they care about is whether she loves them enough to be with them most of the time. "A home must be very bad before it can be bettered by a good institution," writes renowned psychiatrist John Bowlby.[7]

This theory goes back many years. In the movie *Gone With the Wind* (released in the 1930s), Rhett Butler takes his daughter on an extended trip to get her away from Scarlett, a spoiled, petulant woman who made a terrible mother. Rhett was clearly the better parent, and he thought he was doing right by getting his daughter away from her mother. Several weeks into the trip, however, his daughter wanted to go home. She missed her mother terribly. When Rhett returns, he says to Scarlett, "Apparently, any mother—even a bad mother—is better than no mother at all."[8]

But today's parents are told children are better off away from any mother who isn't June Cleaver. "Researchers found that the more dissatisfied a woman was with her home life, the more depressed she tended to be. Conversely, working women felt less depressed about troubles at home than did housewives," writes Susan Chira.[9] It is this assertion that resulted in the infamous claim, "I'm a better mom for working." It is true if a mother is depressed, her attitude and behavior will negatively affect those around her. But to suggest depressed at-home mothers are in any way the norm or that at-home motherhood, in and of itself, makes women more susceptible to depression (postpartum period notwithstanding) is a reach.

There are many reasons why a woman at home may be dissatisfied. Chira presumes a woman's depression has to do with her motherhood role when it's much more likely to be related to her marriage. And though work may seem like an obvious solution, what she will find in most cases is that she's robbed Peter to pay Paul. She may have solved her immediate woes, but she will later confront a new set of problems as she finds herself moving Johnny from place to place because she's unhappy with the daycare she's chosen. Or when her nanny quits—again. Or when she finds Johnny is showing signs of behavior problems. Or when she finds that her stress level has escalated because she has no time for herself, her friends or her husband.

She may find that being a little restless at home wasn't so bad.

One possible solution for women who believe they'd be unhappy at home is to find their children one dependable caregiver who'll stick with the family for the long haul. "Children need one stable adult they can depend on, and their emotional development depends more on having such a person than it does on that person being the mother," writes Hope Edelman in *Mother of My Mother*.[10]

It would be lovely, of course, if our society could count on this kind of solution for such women. But alas, most women cannot afford Mary Poppins. And even if they could, there aren't enough to go around. As Karl Zinsmeister, editor of *American Enterprise*, writes, "In a perfect world, there would be an abundance of intelligent, well-balanced, devoted individuals willing to attend lavishly and patiently to the demands of strangers' children— enough so that every family who wanted could have their own full-time loving surrogate."[11] Alas, this is not reality. It is extraordinarily difficult to find this one very special human being. And when mothers can't find her, they settle for come-and-go nannies and countless daycare providers.

That's when the real problems begin, for the constant merry-go-round of caregivers is the single most destructive outcome of full-time substitute care for children. "The greatest fear for a child is the loss of a primary relationship," writes Dr. Stanley I. Greenspan in *The Irreducible Needs of Children*."[12] Since substitute care is so prevalent, however, we dismiss this fact. Parents ignore the voice in their heads that tells them otherwise. As one woman tells Katherine Goldman about the nanny she chose for her children, "I had a funny twinge about her when she came to us, but I was desperate, and she was good enough, I thought."[13]

Good enough?

Parents must stop and think about what it is they're doing. Does it make sense that a child won't be affected emotionally from bonding with someone and then having that person disappear again and again? (And unless grandma is taking over, this *will* be your baby's fate.) Does it make sense that a child is going to get the same level of care in a group setting than he would one-on-one? Does it make sense that his needs will be met if there are thirty other kids whose needs also must be met, or if he has to convey his needs over and over again to a new caregiver? Does it make sense that his cognitive abilities will be fostered if he has to engage in pre-planned activities as opposed to doing what he's naturally inclined toward? Does it make sense that he will feel as though he is worthy of being heard if he spends years waiting in line?

Of course not. It's inevitable such an environment will have negative effects. We don't always see these effects right away, so we pretend they're not there. It's like the kitchen floor that hasn't been mopped in weeks. It doesn't look too bad at the time and seems to be holding up without a good cleaning, but it isn't until we acknowledge that it needs attention and wash it that we realize how much dirt has accumulated.

It could be years before people are aware of the damage of daycare. "Some youngsters learn not to attach themselves to any caregiver. They lose the ability to feel or express warmth, and develop a shallow and indiscriminate emotional life. Certain such children end up without any sense of personal connectedness," writes Zinsmeister.[14] And because this outcome is so difficult to quantify, many childcare advocates ignore its reality. For if we cannot measure the harmful effects of substitute care ("Johnny is reading below grade level") then there must not be any harm. But there is.

Nannies

Nannies are the least common form of alternative childcare—employed by only 2.4 percent of families with children below the age of five—for good reason: they're expensive. Moreover, searching for a qualified nanny is like finding a needle in a haystack. If more women could afford nannies, and if finding good ones were not so difficult, I think it's fair to assume most families who want care for their children would prefer this solution to daycare.

The most obvious reason is nannies can provide children with the one-on-one attention they need. It's also easier to have someone come to your home than it is to drive children to a daycare center every day. And of course, children who are raised at home won't get sick as often as they would in daycare and can live according to their own schedules and sleep in the comfort of their own rooms.

But there are hidden problems associated with nannies. Perhaps the biggest shock is the realization that nannies just don't stick around. Many mothers find themselves hiring a handful of women since a nanny's job is almost always temporary. As Linda Burton discovered after her years-long search for the perfect nanny, "Many of us nanny-seekers must have acquired vastly sentimentalized notions from old English books or PBS television series that a typical nanny came to change the diapers and stayed on for weddings. The reality was that few modern-day nannies stuck around long enough to see a baby move into toddlerhood."[15] And each time a mother changes providers, her child experiences a significant loss—for the most important factor in a child's development, besides a mother's influence, is having the consistent care and attention of one individual. When the child loses that person, it is huge.

Even when a mother is fortunate enough to find one long-term caregiver, perhaps a family member, she will still confront a host of problems. Her children will probably be more attached to the nanny and will be more likely to listen to and abide by the rules of the nanny. And if the discipline style of the nanny differs from the mother's, and it almost always does, it's going to become a huge issue for the family. When this happens, a mother has to decide whether or not to change nannies. Her gut instinct will tell her this isn't a good idea, but she also believes her children shouldn't receive mixed messages.

In her search for an answer, she may be unfortunate enough to come across articles like "Right Nanny, Wrong Time" in *Working Mother* magazine, which asserts that at times like these—when mothers and nannies conflict—women just have to face the fact that their children need a new nanny. "It's heart-wrenching to admit that a perfect relationship has to come to an end. We go into denial; we turn the other way when established rules begin to slide. Anything but recognize the truth."[16] The truth being, according to the article, that the mother has no choice but to switch caregivers. But the real truth is that which *Working Mother* will never concede: yanking this woman from her children's lives is just about the worst thing she can do. In other words, there *is* no solution to this mother's problem.

Mothers who hire nannies must also face the fact that their nannies know their children better than they do. Peggy Orenstein tells of one working mother who felt "just the tiniest bit threatened" by her nanny.[16] Her nanny told the mother she thought one of the boys in her charge was getting too selfish and that he should take on more of the household chores. The mother said that at first she was put off because she felt she knew her son better than anyone. But then she realized her nanny was right. She finally admitted her nanny spent the most time with her son—over ten hours a day—so she probably knew him better than she did. Such is the price of maternal absence.

Daycare

On October 19, 2000, Katie Couric of the *Today show* interviewed Ellen Galinsky, president of the Families and Work Institute and author of the book *Ask the Children*. The focus of the segment was whether or not daycare was good for children. After Galinsky told Couric she thought daycare could be a positive experience for children—helping them learn leadership skills, for example—Couric asked her whether she thought there were any downsides to daycare. Galinsky responded hesitantly, "Well, yes, daycare can be harmful." Then Couric asked her how it could be harmful. To which Galinsky responded, "Well, when it isn't good." Couric then asked her what percentage of daycare centers *are* considered good.

Galinsky answered, "About 12 percent."[17]

When it comes to the subject of daycare, the most powerful voices in America once again prevail. Most of the information the public receives about daycare is from daycare *advocates*. One would have to do his or her own research to find material that proves the harmful effects of daycare—not because it doesn't exist but because it's not the side of the debate the media wants to address. Consequently, the public is never exposed to an honest, fair debate about daycare.

"Academics, pediatricians, and other experts have learned to keep a prudent silence about the risks of daycare, and so it is the daycare advocates—and only the advocates—we hear from on our television screens and in our parenting magazines," writes Fisher.[18] Many women assume that because pediatricians aren't crying out against daycare, their silence must mean consent. But it doesn't. The only reason pediatricians say nothing is because if they *were* to speak their minds, they'd lose patients. So in a way, they're stuck. It doesn't mean they think daycare is good—it means they're being political. "Many of these advocates will in private candidly concede a gap between their personal values and what they endorse professionally. But in public, you hear only the most unblinking loyalty," adds Fisher.[18]

Which is why Ellen Galinsky can't see the irony in her statement to Couric. She smiles and discusses how daycare can be a wonderful thing for children but glosses over the fact that *eighty-eight percent* of daycare is barely adequate or downright awful! Women like Galinsky, who have an agenda, remain in thrall to the idea that daycare could be great if only there were more funding. But money can never fix a system that is rife with dysfunction at its very core. "America suffers a growing national epidemic of parental absence and disconnection. 'Quality' in day care cannot solve the problem. It doesn't even address it," writes Fisher.[19]

It is unreasonable for Americans to believe the government has the power to make thousands of daycare centers effective. The leaders of the Family and Home Network, an organization that supports the needs of at-home mothers, expressed this point at a hearing before the US House of Representatives. "Seldom do 'more' and 'quality' go hand in hand. If the current childcare experiences we hear about from many former and current working mothers is an accurate indication of the kind of childcare most mothers are finding, then perhaps the attempt to create more daycare merely hits the symptom rather than the root of the problem."[20]

This makes sense, doesn't it? We all know the difference between the quality of service we get at our local, privately owned grocery or hardware store and at a national food chain or Home Depot. So how is it that we believe children can be raised just as well—or even half as well—in a system that is so large, so overwhelming, that its environment can't be controlled?

Even Dr. Stanley Greenspan, author of *The Irreducible Needs of Children*, has said America has struggled to improve daycare for twenty years, without success, and that the only way it *could* be improved is for parents to provide most of their own care for their children. That way, there would be fewer people using daycare and perhaps then it could have a fighting chance. In the meantime, we've convinced ourselves that daycare is harmless.

That which we desire most earnestly, we believe most easily.

On April 20, 2001, the most significant government-sponsored daycare research to date was released by Dr. Jay Belsky, who first sparked debate fifteen years ago when he suggested daycare posed a risk to children with developmental problems. This new research supported his previous position. "We find clearly, indisputably, and unambiguously that the more time children spend in daycare, the more likely they are to be aggressive and disobedient," he said.[21] The report also found that the results are the same regardless of the type or quality of daycare, the sex of the child or whether the family is rich or poor. What matters most is time: the more hours spent away from parents, the more likely children are to have behavioral problems.

Again, sounds reasonable, doesn't it? The research didn't say that the mere exposure to daycare is harmful to children. It said *exceptionally long hours in daycare* are harmful. The research doesn't say that when I go to the gym and drop my daughter off in the nursery for an hour while I take an aerobics class that I'm causing her harm, but it does point out that if I left her there all day, every day, it *would* be harmful.

Naturally, childcare advocates dispute Belsky's research. In an interview with Dan Rather, Marion Wright Edelman, president of the National Children's Defense Fund, said, "This is an opportunity not just to blame daycare but to improve daycare, and not to blame parents but to make it easier for parents to balance their work and family needs." When Rather asked Edelman for her response to those who would say the research is evidence that daycare just doesn't work, she replied, "Well, there's no evidence that daycare just doesn't work."[22]

That which we desire most earnestly, we believe most easily.

Galinksy also questions the research—not surprisingly, since it disputes the findings in her book *Ask the Children*—by arguing that the number of hours children are away from their mothers really isn't what matters. What matters is whether a mother is stressed and tired when she returns home in the evening. If the mother is able to separate her work life from her home life, there is no cause for concern. But who isn't stressed and tired after a day at the office? Moreover, it was Galinsky's organization (the Families and Work Institute) that did the research that found it was *more* likely a mother's work life would intrude on her home life rather than the other way around.

The claims of childcare advocates notwithstanding, research shows most Americans do not support daycare and believe parents are the best source of care for children. "We examined the attitudes of parents with young children, employers, and children's advocates on the issue of childcare and what society should do about it. We found solid consensus on what people consider most desirable: a parent at home, either mother or father, at least for the first years of a child's life."[23]

Ironically, many daycare providers themselves don't support daycare! I spoke with the director of a childcare center who has worked in daycare for over five years. She told me she has let parents know that while her center provides children with the best possible care, it is still second best. She then said she has no intention of using daycare when she has children. It isn't surprising childcare providers would feel this way— they know best the conditions in most daycare centers and how children cope in that environment. Unfortunately, most aren't forthcoming because they need their jobs.

The real problem with daycare is that few people are willing to tell the truth about what they know. Others remain blissfully unaware. There's also no accurate, objective way to measure the evidence. Ellen Galinsky's book, *Ask the Children: What America's Children Really Think About Working Parents*, is a perfect example. It has been hailed as "groundbreaking" since it is the first book to gather information on how children feel about the fact that their parents work. The implication is that asking the kids makes the findings more accurate. But children are blindly devoted to their parents and are thus unable to be objective.

They also don't know any experience other than their own and hence consider their own experiences to be normal. Trying to determine how a mother's work affects children by asking the children themselves is absurd. How can we expect children to assess the sociological implications of our decisions when even we adults can't? Take, for example, Galinsky's quote from a fifteen-year-old girl whose parents both work full-time: "It's okay to work. The kid is going to turn out the same way if you work, or if you don't work."[24]

This response may appease parents, but it doesn't prove anything except what we want it to prove. Just to emphasize how misinformed children are, consider this statement from an eighteen-year-old girl: "The only thing I hope I do when I am a parent is to get a career I love so everything would be easier."[25] There you have it: we've somehow managed to teach young girls that "getting a career" when they become mothers will help make life *easier* for them.

Childcare advocates love to stress the idea that children whose parents both work "turn out fine." This can certainly be true, but it is once again impossible to gather the kind of information one would need to determine whether or not a person "turned out fine." There's simply no way to measure this. What do we mean when we say a person "turns out fine"? Whether or not a child who was raised in daycare gets an education or a job, or whether or not he gets married and has a family, tells us nothing. It's the intangibles that matter. The child's ability to trust others, for example. Or to be vulnerable, or to get along with others, or to persevere when things get tough—these are things that cannot be measured.

How do you determine how much baggage a person has? "It's difficult to measure many of the most important emotional capacities, such as intimacy, sense of self, and future capacities to parent and nurture children," writes Greenspan.[26] Trying to determine whether or not a child "turns out fine" is very difficult: there are just too many variables. That's why it's so important for women to listen to their instincts—and yes, even their guilt—and use common sense when it comes to daycare. They must turn a deaf ear to those who, because of a need to rationalize their commitment to childcare, create bogus theories about what children need.

Some, for example, insist daycare teaches children how to be independent. "Children [in high-quality daycare] are stronger leaders, more independent and more self-confident," says daycare provider Bobbie Noonan.[27] But thrusting a baby into daycare does not create an independent nature—that is a gradual process. "To develop into an emotionally healthy person, your child needs to progress through the stages gradually. Moving from dependency to being able to do things independently is challenging, and requires your patience and support."[28]

In other words, parents must first meet their babies' need for *de*pendence before they can even think about a child becoming independent. As William and Wendy Dreskin, former childcare directors and authors of *The Day Care Decision*, write, "Children who are nourished by love feel secure and have the easiest time when the 'famine' of separation hits. But children who have been deprived since infancy have no reserves to fall back on."[29]

This has been known for some time. In 1962, the US Department of Health, Education, and Welfare's Office of Child Development published a booklet entitled "Your Child From 1 to 6." In the section on babies and toddlers, it reads:

If [the toddler] continues to receive the warm assurance he has had, he will grow more sure of himself. If he is pushed out faster than he is ready to go, he will always be a little less confident, and a little more dependent on others than he might otherwise have been. These early experiences have a lifelong effect. Even though the child doesn't remember what actually happened, and lacks words to give it shape in his mind, the feelings remain. He learns that he can count on people—or that he cannot; that he will be allowed to try things out—or that he'll be constantly thwarted. These characteristic ways of looking at things tend to persist and become a fixed part of the personality.

In other words, daycare produces the *opposite* effect of what childcare advocates claim. Developing independence, or even overcoming shyness, can't be remedied by putting a child in daycare because that environment is not how children gain a sense of self. What childcare advocates call independence, you and I might see as something else. As Jeree Pawl, director of the infant-parent program at the University of California-San Francisco said, "In most daycare centers, it's a pecking order; it's like a bunch of wild chickens in a hen yard."[30] The result is that "the loudest and most obnoxious behavior is what gets rewarded with attention from overloaded adult caretakers and intimidated peers," writes Karl Zinsmeister.[31]

A child can become independent in any number of ways, and how this trait manifests itself in his or her personality is key. "It is the quality of a child's independence that concerns most mothers: Was it born of necessity or self-confidence? Do their children know they can make it on their own because they're rich in resources or because, by golly, they had to? Can they help other people along the way because somebody took the time to help them or do they ignore the needs of other people because no one was there when they had a need? Will they be able to combat any potential challenges because they feel nurtured, secure in themselves and their abilities or because they had to fight to get it?" writes Linda Burton.[32]

Parents have also been taught that babies and toddlers require stimulation mothers can't provide. That's the impetus for another rationalization about daycare: the idea that babies need daycare in order to be intellectually stimulated. Not only is this clinically false, it's silly. As one working mother tells Betty Holcomb, "Daycare turned out to be an enriching experience for me and my son. At ten weeks old, he was coming home with artwork."[33]

Too many parents are unaware that *the single greatest factor* in the life of a newborn is emotional attachment. Not only is intellectual development secondary, it's practically irrelevant. "We must remember it is the emotional development of the infant that forms the foundation upon which all later achievements are based. For the infant, a mother is the environment—pre-natally and post-natally. As a society, we are uncomfortable admitting this—but it is a biological fact," writes Fisher.[34]

In other words, trying to develop a baby's intellect with the help of specially designed toys or creative projects is useless. The ordinary kitchen utensils in our cupboards will engage babies more than anything we can buy for them at Toys 'R Us. The way a baby learns and grows is by watching his mother (or alternate caregiver) day in and day out. Consistency and repetition is the one thing that truly does help foster their intellect.

Then there's the notorious issue of socialization. Obviously children want and need to socialize—the question is when and in what form they need it. Babies don't socialize. The playgroups moms join are for the mothers' benefit, not the newborns'. It isn't until children are older, around two years old, that they begin to engage in parallel play with other children. And even then it isn't necessary; it's just fun. It only becomes necessary around the age of three.

I'm reminded of a baby shower I attended. As we all know, baby showers comprise two generations of women: the friends of the woman who's having a baby, who are usually in their twenties or thirties, and the friends of the woman's mother. At this particular shower, the younger set was mostly made up of working mothers, while the older set had been home with their children. I remember two distinct conversations, one with the younger set and one with the older set.

In the conversation with working mothers, an attorney with a three-year-old daughter in daycare told us she was in the middle of a job change. She said she had been laid off from her job and was currently collecting unemployment. When another mother asked how things were going at home with her daughter, she replied confidently that her daughter was still in daycare. She said she was working on various projects at home and really "loves her daughter's daycare center because it provides her with great stimulation." She adds, "There's just no way I could provide her with the stimulation she needs."

That which we desire most earnestly, we believe most easily.

Fast forward about an hour. I was sitting at a table with the older generation, and one of the mothers told a story about her daughter having run away when she was six years old because she was convinced that her mother was the worst mother in the world. So she packed her bags, winter coat and all—even though it was summertime—and took off down the street. The woman told us she knew where her daughter was headed, so she called her neighbor whose daughter was the same age as her own. While she was on the phone, she heard her daughter stomp into the neighbor's house crying, telling her friend how mean her mother was and wondering if she could live there with them. The two mothers hung up, and the neighbor told the girl that, yes, certainly she could live with them. She said they had room in the basement with a very comfortable bed and bath.

The girl was very happy and proceeded to unpack her belongings. Then the mother handed the girl a dust cloth and told her she'd have to earn her keep by helping the mother clean the house every day. In less than half an hour, the girl was gone. It seems her mother wasn't so bad after all. As I sat there listening to this woman's story, I thought about days long gone: when mothers were around, soaking up every delightful bit of their children's nonsense—and about how women were around to help each other out. Then I thought of the attorney and wondered if she had any idea what she was giving up.

The lies parents tell themselves about why they work have no end. One woman tells Arlie Hochschild that her son Nicky is in daycare from eight in the morning to five in the evening every day, but since she likes to work out at the gym twice a week, she makes sure to have her husband or sister pick him up for her so he doesn't have to stay at daycare until six. After all, she says, "I don't see why some parents have kids if they don't want to take care of them." Here's a woman who honestly believes she's doing something great by refusing to let her son stay in daycare one extra hour twice a week. In her mind, five nine-hour days—forty-five hours a week—seems reasonable. But forty-seven hours just wouldn't be right.

Others insist there's no difference between a child who's raised at home and a child who's raised in daycare as long as Mom is a "sensitive, responsive, and caring parent" during the time she does spend with her children, says Holcomb.[35] That's like saying there's no difference between an employee who comes to work every day and does the job and an employee who only shows up one day a week—but on that particular day is really useful. The truth is, "young children do not form a strong attachment to a person they see little of, no matter how kindly the person is or how superlative the quality of time spent together," write William and Wendy Dreskin.[36]

One at-home mother addressed this point online to family therapist Gayle Peterson. The mother writes that she's frustrated with media reports that say it doesn't matter whether or not she's home with her children: "How can it be that children are not negatively affected when they only see their parents two hours each day?"[37] The answer Peterson gives is the standard feel good response: that, ultimately, whatever works best for this mother is what matters the most. Then she implies working motherhood is ultimately beneficial because "no child benefits from a mother who never develops any interests or activities outside of her children"[38]—as though being employed is the only way a mother can pursue her other interests and talents. Still, Peterson is quick to add that this mother should not devalue the work she does at home because "it is priceless."[39]

The problem with Peterson's response, which is typical of childcare advocates, is that it's contradictory. You can't say in one breath that there's no difference between the child who's raised at home and the child who isn't and also say at-home motherhood is "priceless." If mothering is "priceless," or such an important job we can't put a price on it, how can it make little difference whether mothers stay home and perform this work? Peterson doesn't answer the woman's question at all. Instead she dances around it, using politically correct jargon to evade the fact that the woman is right: of *course* there's a difference between a child who's raised at home and a child who's raised in daycare.

A final rationalization is the claim that children "love daycare," that they can't wait to get there and never want to leave. For one thing, the average toddler is not getting up at seven in the morning and bounding off to daycare. And children who appear enthused are often putting on an act. A child's unwillingness to go home with his mother at the end of the day because he's having so much fun isn't good. Children are attracted to what they know, for they have nothing with which to compare their experience. So if a child has always been in daycare, then daycare is where the child is most comfortable. Daycare *is* home, so of course they want to be there.

It's not our children's job to know what's good for them—it's our job as their parents. A child may say he loves daycare, but he also loves candy. Does this mean we should let him eat it all day, every day? Children also don't think they're tired when they really are (which is why their initial reaction to naptime and bedtime is a resounding "No!"). Should we let them stay up? No, because we know they're tired even though they don't think they are. We know that once their heads hit the pillow, they'll be asleep. That's why we're the parents and they're the children.

Do not assume children who say they love daycare are happy there. "Children will become reconciled to their fate. They may stop expressing themselves to the daycare workers and their parents, but their feelings have not evaporated. Once children have realized that complaints in any form consistently bring censure, even if they are directly questioned they will dutifully repeat that they like daycare," write the Dreskins.[40]

* * *

A common misperception about mothers at home is that many of these women believe their children should never be separated from them. But most full-time moms agree it's healthy for them and their children to be apart on occasion. It's a matter of how long and how often children should be away from their mothers.

Many at-home moms use their local Mom's Day Out program, which is designed to give parents a break and give their children a chance to explore the world without them. Many mothers also use the nursery at their local gym. These settings bear a striking resemblance to daycare. The difference is the amount of time children spend there: an average of maybe five hours per week. That's just enough time for children to explore the world outside their doorstep but not so long they begin to get anxious looking for Mom.

The most powerful voices in America have an obligation to warn parents of the detriments of daycare, and they aren't doing it. Instead they talk about how daycare has the potential to be good one day and offer suggestions about how mothers can improve the quality of care their children are receiving, as though working mothers have any control over what happens when they're not around. Here's Ellen Galinsky's suggestion: "There's always something you can do. Maybe just bring a book to a provider so she can read to your child. Say something that makes her more interested in her job. If we want better for our children, change is not going to be handed to us. We have to make it happen."[41]

Instead of women getting the message that the only way to ensure that their children will get the best care is to raise them at home, they get the message that they can help their children get what they need by trying to alter the emotional outlook of their children's transient daycare provider.

That which we desire most earnestly, we believe most easily.

For the record, none of this is to suggest daycare shouldn't exist at all. We just need perspective. Daycare originally began as a Head Start program designed to help low-income families by providing a place for them to keep their children safe while the parents went to work. But no one thought to argue that this environment was *preferable* to the home.

The daycare of today has little to do with this initial plan for alternative childcare. Today daycare is open to anyone who wants to use it. It has become a parent's right, rather than a last resort for those who've exhausted every other means to care for their children. As Karl Zinsmeister observes, "there's a difference between a compromise made in reaction to some crisis of fate and an arrangement made simply because one wants to maximize one's own position while ignoring serious costs to others."[42]

It's disturbing how immune we've become to daycare. Children don't thrive in daycare—they get used to it. Children will get used to anything we ask them to; that's why our power is so frightening. But when children are left in daycare eight to ten hours a day, all week long, the only thing they take away from the experience is that there's someplace else their parents would rather be.

CONCLUSION

THE WAY FORWARD

As I gazed out into the comic fog of my motherhood, I began to wonder if maybe there wasn't a lesson in this for me. Maybe motherhood was an opportunity to face certain things that, under normal circumstances, I'd want to avoid. Like sitting. And just being. I realized that motherhood's commitment was an opportunity for me to peel back some of my life's more surfacey layers and have a peek at what I was really made of.

— *Laurie Wagner*

In 1999, $500 million dollars' worth of self-help books was sold.[1] *Five hundred million dollars.* Seems to me if what feminists said were true, that getting women out of the home and into the workforce would make them happier, women would be too busy being joyous to scour the self-help section of the bookstore. "I don't think women as a group are much happier now than they were in the 50s," admits psychologist Mary Pipher.[2]

They are not; the reason is that women don't want their professional accomplishments to come *at the expense of* motherhood. That's the underlying issue. What most women want is to be successful at work and at home. And they can be. But not if they follow the cultural script feminists have laid out for women.

Look, I get it. I understand the pull between work and home—I sometimes feel I have more ambition than I know what to do with. But like most women, I've curbed this ambition in order to raise a family. We never talk about this because that would be taboo. In postfeminist America, a woman is viewed as incomplete if her ambition isn't embraced full throttle.

It's time for that nonsense to change. Most women are some combination of "working mother" and "stay at home mother." When looking at their lives as a whole, women want to be wives and mothers as well as independent workers. Most of us make choices every day about how to make this happen. If I didn't have children, I'd have a completely different life. My husband and I probably wouldn't choose to live where we do (St. Louis is a great place to raise kids), and work would be the focus of my life—just as it was prior to having children. And when my children are grown and gone, I expect my life will look like that again.

When we choose to have children, we choose a new life. We choose a life of trade-offs. That's why the idea of 'having it all,' at least at the same time, is bogus. Women *can* have most of what they want over the course of their lives, but they'll need to adjust their expectations. And they'll need to broaden their view of what it means to be successful.

I was fortunate to have received this message early on. Most of the women in my family are highly educated yet still managed to incorporate at-home motherhood into their lives. They did this in various ways. Some married early and started their careers later; some postponed marriage and had long careers beforehand; and some quit working once they saw how challenging it was to balance career and family and modified their plans accordingly.

Because of their example, I've always known I would have both work and motherhood in my life. But never once did I consider doing both at the same time. Nor did I get the idea that an educated woman can't be bothered with caring for babies— that she either gets an education and pursues a career *or* she raises kids. But I did get the message that 'having it all' at once was not the way to go.

It's so important for women to absorb this early on, for if there's one thing young women want to know, it's how they will balance work and family when the time comes. The answer is sequencing. When women sequence their lives, or plan for the various seasons of a woman's life, they make space for both work and family.

In other words, women should assume the opposite of what they do now. Assume you *will* be at home with your children for a period of time and will thus be out of the workforce awhile— perhaps up to 10 years, depending on the number of children you have. That's not how women are taught to map out their lives. They're taught to assume a job will be the focus of their lives, and children will magically orbit around it. They're being set up to fail—because that is not at all what happens.

So how does a woman sequence her life? First, choose a career that works well with motherhood. In the past, women chose professions like nursing and teaching in large part because these jobs are flexible. Flexibility is key.

What about those careers that don't offer women the flexibility they want? That is a quandary, no doubt. The choice to pursue a demanding career will come at a cost. Those who pursue such careers pay a big price for their achievement in the long hours they must commit to their careers. That is the nature of the game.

The second component of sequencing is for women to live near their families of origin once they have children. Women need help when their babies arrive! Millions of mothers are exasperated today because no one's around to help them. Some can substitute with friends, and some women have enough money to pay for babysitters or nannies. But most do not. That's when family help becomes priceless.

The third requirement is to be smart with one's money prior to motherhood. One of the reasons people say families need two incomes is because couples got used to living the good life prior to having children. I know the idea is to "live it up" before you settle down—get all those trips in, etc.—but saving money prior to motherhood, or just being more frugal, helps alleviate the blow couples face in having to lower their standard of living after they become parents.

The final requirement of sequencing is for women to choose a husband who works full-time at a job adequate to meet the family's needs. Too many women today disregard a man's work prospects. They view men as their "equals" and thus assume both of them will work full-time and year-round after having children. But many women come to regret this since it doesn't allow them even the option to stay home. They bought into the lie that looking for a husband to support his wife at all, even for a short time, is backward.

You might be thinking that not all jobs or careers can be ditched for a period of time only to be returned to later, and that is true. But that is a decision women have to make based on their priorities. Everything we do comes at a price. If you bow out of a career in your 30s, you'll be less likely to make it to the top of your field. But the alternative is to land the corner office and not be close to your children or be the "go-to" adult in their lives. That's what trade-offs are all about.

* * *

It's time to shift our paradigm. Unless a big career is your ultimate goal in life, there's no reason you need to do everything at once. Women have plenty of time to be mothers and to pursue their other interests and passions. "Just as the young never really understand, or believe, that there is a long, long time stretching ahead of them in which to do all the things they want, so many young mothers continue to feel that if they don't move on the question of career now, the world will simply pass them by," writes Midge Decter.[3]

The trick is to get beyond the need to prove your value to the world, for that is how this madness began. Feminists sabotaged motherhood. Women in the past weren't expected to earn an income in order to prove their value because it was plainly evident that what they were doing was of value. That is no longer the case.

By demeaning motherhood, the only way women can earn respect is to get a job. But women who want to be happy are going to have to ignore the culture and listen to their gut. If happiness is the goal, and let's assume it is, for most women being career-focused won't make that happen. It is our relationships at home that reveal how happy or unhappy we truly are.

Quality of life matters, too. Anyone who has read the behind-the-scenes life of a typical dual-income family can see for themselves how crazy that life is. Here's an example, taken from the cover story of a recent issue of *Time* magazine.

It's 6:35 in the morning, and Cheryl Nevins, 34, dressed for work in a silky black maternity blouse and skirt, is busily tending to Ryan, 2 1/2, and Brendan, 11 months, at their home in the leafy Edgebrook neighborhood of Chicago. Both boys are sobbing because Reilly, the beefy family dog, knocked Ryan over. In a blur of calm, purposeful activity, Nevins, who is 8 months pregnant, shoves the dog out into the backyard, changes Ryan's diaper on the family-room rug, heats farina in the microwave and feeds Brendan cereal and sliced bananas while crooning Open, Shut Them to encourage the baby to chew. Her husband Joe, 35, normally out the door by 5:30 a.m. for his job as a finance manager for Kraft Foods, makes a rare appearance in the morning muddle. "I do want to go outside with you," he tells Ryan, who is clinging to his leg, "but

Daddy has to work every day except Saturdays and Sundays. That stinks."

At 7:40, Vera Orozco, the nanny, arrives to begin her 10 1/2-hour shift at the Nevinses'. Cheryl, a labor lawyer for the Chicago board of education, hands over the baby and checks her e-mail from the kitchen table. "I almost feel apprehensive if I leave for work without logging on," she confesses. Throughout the day, Orozco will note every meal and activity on a tattered legal pad on the kitchen counter so Nevins can stay up to speed.

It is important for couples to know ahead of time that this is what the quality of their lives will look like if they both choose to work full-time, particularly when their children are young. And the above scenario doesn't even factor in the stress from commuting, or the conflict about how dinner is going to get on the table, or the fights over who's going to do what, etc. When making decisions about work and family, we need to factor in the intangibles. A second income isn't advantageous if the flipside means living a life of chaos and discord. It just isn't worth it.

It seems to me the secret of this conversation is the ability to look forward, into the future. If you know you want children, you should know they will change the entire course of your life. It comes down to prioritizing your non-negotiables. For me, there was never any question that I wanted children and that I'd be home with them. That meant all other decisions I made—what to study in school, what kind of job to pursue, whom to marry, where to live—were tailored around that central goal. This has made, thus far anyway, all the difference in the world.

Does my being at home ensure my daughter will become a perfect child? Of course not. But it does mean she knows I'll be here for her tomorrow. And the next day. And the day after that. It means she can count on me not to be a perfect mother but a stable force in her life. Most important, it means she knows I consider her worth my time and attention.

And this will mark her soul for a lifetime.

ENDNOTES

Chapter 1: Go Ahead: Let Down the Sisterhood

1 Christina Hoff Sommers, *Who Stole Feminism? How Women Have Betrayed Women* (New York: Simon and Schuster, 1994), 17.

2 Sommers writes that "gender feminists" believe all our institutions perpetuate male dominance.

3 F. Carolyn Graglia, *Domestic Tranquility: A Brief Against Feminism* (Dallas: Spence Publishing, 1998), 4.

4 Betty Friedan, *The Feminine Mystique* (New York: W.W. Norton & Company, 2001), xv.

5 Ibid.

6 Ibid., xvi.

7 Midge Decter, *An Old Wife's Tale: My Seven Decades In Love and War* (New York: Regan Books, 2001), 92.

8 Friedan, 317.

9 Ann Crittenden, 13.

10 Interview with Marlo Thomas on The Phil Donahue Show (1970s), as seen on *Lifetime* television.

11 Megan Rutherford, "When Mother Stays Home," *Time. com* (October 16, 2000).

12 Sylvia Ann Hewlett, *Creating a Life: Professional Women and the Quest for Children* (New York: Hyperion, 2002), 119-20.

13 Lisa Schiffren, "Family First," *Wall Street Journal* (March 19, 1998): A18.

14 Peggy Orenstein, *Flux: Women on Sex, Work, Love, Kids, & Life In a Half-Changed World* (New York: Anchor Books, 2000), 17.

15 Susan Douglas and Meredith Michaels, *The Mommy Myth: The Idealization of Motherhood and How It Has Undermined Women* (New York: Free Press, 2004), 34.

Chapter 2: 7 Myths about Staying Home

1   Friedan, 377.

2   Danielle Crittenden, *What Our Mothers Didn't Tell Us: Why Happiness Eludes the Modern Woman* (New York: Touchstone, 1999), 121.

3   Decter, 193.

4   Telephone Interview (October 2001)

5   Rutherford, "When Mother Stays Home"

6   Ann Crittenden, 72.

7   United States Census Bureau Current Population Survey, March 1997.

8   Lisa Collier Cool, "Raising Kids in a World of Internet Speed," *Child* (August 2001): 76.

9   Linda Burton, Janet Dittmer, and Cheri Loveless, *What's a Smart Woman Like You Doing At Home?* (Vienna, VA: Family and Home Network, 1992), 132.

10 Meghan Cox Gurdon, "She's Back!" *The Women's Quarterly* (Spring 1998)

11 Gurdon, "She's Back!"

12 Gurdon, "She's Back!"

13 Gurdon, "She's Back!"

14 Hewlett, 83-4.

15 Burton, Dittmer, and Loveless, 63.

16 Joan K. Peters, *When Mothers Work: Loving Our Children Without Sacrificing Ourselves* (New York: Addison Wesley Longman, 1997), xiii.

17 Maria Shriver, *Ten Things (I Wish I'd Known — Before I Went Out into the Real World)*. (New York: Warner Books, 2000), 81.

18 Friedan, 381.

19 Susan Chira, *A Mother's Place: Choosing Work and Family Without Guilt or Blame* (New York: Harper Collins, 1998), xiii.

20 Ibid., 46.

21 Ibid., 23.

22 Orenstein, 33.

23 Arlie Russell Hochschild, *The Time Bind: When Work Becomes Home & Home Becomes Work* (New York: Metropolitan, 1997), 186.

24 Shannon Brownlee and Matthew Miller, "Lies Parents Tell Themselves About Why They Work," *U.S News & World Report* (May 12, 1997): 59.

25 Goldberg, 61.

26 Ibid., 59.

27 Ibid., 167.

28 Freidan, xv.

Chapter 3: The Two-Income Trap

1 Jennifer Roback Morse, "Why the Market Can't Raise Our Children for Us," *American Enterprise* (May/June 1998).

2 Danielle Crittenden, 132-33.

3 Brownlee and Miller, 60.

4 Ibid.

5 David Brooks, "Why the US Will Always Be Rich," *The New York Times Magazine* (June 9, 2002.)

6 Ibid.

7 Peggy Orenstein, "Will Your Child Suffer If You Work?" *Redbook* (August 2001): 55.

8 Stephen Covey, *The 7 Habits of Highly Effective Families* (New York: Golden Books, 1997), 118.

9 Ibid.

10 Brownlee and Miller, 59.

11 Decter, 50.

12 Oprah Winfrey, Interview with the Dalai Lama, *O, The Oprah Magazine* (August 2001): 123.

13 Robert Reich, *The Future of Success* (New York: Alfred Knopf, 2001), 175.

14 Anna Quindlen, *A Short Guide to a Happy Life* (New York: RandomHouse, 2000), 38.

15 *Good Morning America*, June 19, 2002; Daniel McGinn, "Maxed Out!" *Newsweek* (August 27, 2001): 34.

16 Thomas J. Stanley, Ph.D. and William D. Danko, Ph.D., *The Millionaire Next Door: The Surprising Secrets of America's Wealthy* (New York: Simon & Schuster, 1996), 1.

17 Reich, 226.

18 Sue Shellenbarger, "In Cataclysmic Times, Workers

Need Room to Rethink Priorities," *The Wall Street Journal* (September 19, 2001): B1.

19 Burton, Dittmer, and Loveless, 99.

Chapter 4: The Fallout

1 Sue Shellenbarger, "You Can Find the Time," *Parade* (August 5, 2001): 10.

2 Judith Regan, "Quality Time," *O, The Oprah Magazine* (April 2001): 92.

3 Irene Philipson, *Married to the Job* (New York: Atria Books, 2003)

4 Ibid.

5 Karen Levine, "Family Time Band," *Parents* (April 1998): 124.

6 Ibid.

7 Interview with Laura Pappano in *Radcliffe Quarterly* (Summer 2001): 21.

8 Lisa Belkin, *Life's Work* (New York: Simon & Schuster, 2002), 120

9 Susan Maushart, *The Mask of Motherhood: How Becoming a Mother Changes Our Lives and Why We Never Talk About It* (New York: Penguin Books, 1999), 200.

10 Alison Ashton, "When It's Work vs. Family, Work Usually Wins," *Working Mother* (December 2001): 10.

11 Katherine Wyse Goldman, *Working Mothers 101: Working Mothers 101: How to Organize Your Life, Your Children, and Your Career to Stop Feeling Guilty and Start Enjoying It All* (New York: Cliff Street Books, 1998), 4,157.

12 Ibid., 159.

14 Ibid., 160.

15 Ann Crittenden, 22.

16 Friedan, xv.

17 Friedan, xxiv.

18 Friedan, xxiii.

19 Rhonda Kruse Nordin and Dwenda K. Gjerdingen, *After the Baby: Making Sense of Marriage After Childbirth* (Dallas: Taylor Publishing, 2000), 87.

20 Shriver, 78.

21 Ibid.

22 Chira, xv.

23 "How do we make it work?" ed., *St. Louis Post-Dispatch* (October 26, 2000).

24 Goldman, 57.

25 Ibid, 175.

26 Shellenbarger, 10.

27 Ibid.

28 Ibid.

29 Philipson, 46.

30 Orenstein, 201.

31 Katy Abel, "Time Well Spent: Working Moms and Kids," *Family Education.com*.

32 Goldman, 18.

33 Ibid.

34 Ibid.

35 Hochschild, 212.

36 Orenstein, 55.

37 Annie Finnigan, "The Inside Story," *Working Mother* (October 2001): 66.

38 Arlie Hochschild, *The Second Shift: Working Parents and the Revolution At Home* (New York: Viking Press, 1989), 97.

39 Nordin and Gjerdingen, 85.

Chapter 5: Raising Kids in a Rush

1 Susan Caminiti, "Work and Family," *Parenting* (May 2001): 59.

2 Penelope Leach, "The Most Important Bond," *Child* (October 2001): 64.

3 Barbara Kantrowitz and Pat Wingert, "The Parent Trap," *Newsweek* (January 29, 2001): 49.

4 Personal Interview, May 2001.

5 Personal Interview, August 2001.

6 Personal Interview, December 2001; "No more 9 to 5," *Minnesota Monthly* (January 2002).

7 Ron Taffel, *The Second Family: How Adolescent Power Is Changing the American Family* (New York: St. Martin's Press, 2001), 19.

8 Ibid., 20.

9 Inda Schaenen, *The 7 O'Clock Bedtime* (New York: Regan Books, 2001): xii.

10 Dr. Marc Weissbluth, "Sleeping With Ease," *The Today Show* (November 16, 2001)

11 Jodi Mindell, Ph.D., "How Much Sleep Does Your Child Need?" *BabyCenter.com*

12 Diane Fisher, Ph.D., Testimony, "Pre to Three: Policy Implications of Child Brain Development," June 5,1997.

13 Richard Ferber, *Solve Your Child's Sleep Problems* (New York: Fireside Books, 1985).

14 Weissbluth, "Sleeping With Ease"

15 Schaenen, 134.

16 Reich, 159.

17 Goldman,51.

18 Ibid., 52.

19 Nanci Hellmich, "Fingers point to Mom for picky eaters," *USA Today* (February 25, 2002): 13b.

20 Ibid.

21 Shannon Brownlee, "Too Heavy, Too Young," *Time* (January 21, 2002): 88.

22 Ibid.

23 Cynthia Billhartz, "Taste Buds in Training," *St. Louis Post Dispatch* (August 12, 2001): EV1.

24 Brownlee, 89.

25 Billhartz, EV1.

26 Leonard Pitts Jr., "Parents Have to Learn They Can't Be Playmates," *St. Louis Post-Dispatch* (July 28, 2001): 29.

27 Michael Gurian, *The Wonder of Girls: Understanding the Hidden Nature of Our Daughters* (New York: Pocket Books, 2002), 114.

28 Brazelton, T. Berry, M.D. and Greenspan, Stanley I., M.D. *The Irreducible Needs of Children* (Massachusetts: Perseus Publishing, 2000), 146.

29 Gurian, 122.

30 Brazelton and Greenspan, 154.

31 Ibid.

32 Gurdon, "She's Back!"

33 Schaenen, 24.

34 Anna Quindlen, "Doing Nothing is Something" *Time* (May 13, 2002): 76.

35 Schaenen, 25.

36 Susan Sherrod, "Parental involvement, support are key to a child's success in school," *Naples Daily News* (January 20, 2002): b3.

37 Sal Severe, Ph.D., *How To Behave So Your Children Will Too* (New York: Viking Press, 2000), 93.

38 Katie O'Connor, *The Ladue News* (March 2001).

39 Interview with Melinda Southern, The Oprah Show (October 18, 2000).

40 Michele Orecklin, "Off the Couch," *People* (April 15, 2002): 83.

Chapter 6: What Parents Need to Know about Nannies and Daycare

1   Covey, 119.

2   Chira., 164.

3   Ibid., 165.

4   Ibid.

5   Judith Wallerstein, *The Unexpected Legacy of Divorce* (New York: Hyperion, 2001), 98.

6   Fisher, "Pre to Three"

7   Karl Zinsmeister, "The Problem With Day Care," *American Enterprise* (May/June 1998)

8   Clark Gable to Vivien Leigh, *Gone With The Wind* (1939).

9   Chira, 130.

10 Hope Edelman, *Mother of My Mother* (New York: The Dial Press, 1999), 40.

11 Karl Zinsmeister, "The Problem With Day Care."

12 Greenspan, 18.

13 Goldman, 72.

14 Karl Zinsmeister, "The Problem With Day Care."

15 Burton, Dittmer, and Loveless, 49.

16 Nancy Hall, "Right Nanny, Wrong Time," *Working Mother* (July/August, 2001): 74.

17 Interview with Ellen Galinksy, *The Today Show* (October 16, 2000).

18 Fisher, "Pre to Three."

19 Ibid.

20 Ibid.

21 Jay Belsky, NICHD Study (April 2001).

22 Interview with Marion Wright Edelman, CBS Evening News with Dan Rather (2001).

23 Steve Farkas, "Necessary Compromises: How Parents, Employers, and Children's Advocates View Child Care Today," *Public Agenda Online* (August 2000)

24 Ellen Galinsky, *Ask the Children: What America's Children Really Think About Working Parents* (New York: William Morrow & Co., 1999), 332.

25 Ibid., 341.

26 Greenspan, Diane Rehm.

27 Meghan Mutchler Deerin, "Shedding light on the day care doom and gloom," *The Chicago Tribune* (July 15, 2001): 6.

28 "Independence Takes Form," Loving Your Child Every Step of the Way from American Baby, 47.

29 William and Wendy Dreskin, *The Day Care Decision* (New York: M. Evans and Company, Inc., 1983), 50.

30 Zinsmeister, "The Problem With Day Care."

31 Ibid.

32 Burton, Dittmer, and Loveless, 64.

33 Betty Holcomb, *Not Guilty! The Good News for Working Mothers* (New York: Simon & Schuster, 1998), 208.

34 Fisher, "Pre to Three."

35 Holcomb, 20.

36 William and Wendy Dreskin, 72.

37 Gayle Peterson, "Stay-at-home mom frustrated with media," iVillage.com.

38 Ibid.

39 Ibid.

40 William and Wendy Dreskin, 112.

41 Harriet Brown, "Who's Watching Our Children?" *Parenting.com* (June/July 1999)

42 Zinsmeister

Conclusion: The Way Forward

1 Statistic reported on the CBS Nightly News, 2000.

2 Hayes, "Women Seeking Balance"

3 Decter, 58.

ABOUT THE AUTHOR

Suzanne Venker is an author and cultural critic who writes about relationships, marriage, and work–family issues. A nationally recognized expert on America's gender war, she's a contributor at Fox News and appears regularly on *Fox & Friends*. She is also a columnist at PJ Media and a trustee at Leading Women for Shared Parenting, an organization that recognizes children need both parents.

Suzanne's writing has appeared in many publications, including *Time*, *Parents*, the *New York Post*, Heat Street, and the *St. Louis Post-Dispatch;* and her work has been featured in *The Wall Street Journal*, *Newsweek*, *The Atlantic*, *The Economist*, *The Huffington Post*, and London's *Daily Mail*. Her TV credits include *STOSSEL*, *The View*, ABC, CNN, C-Span's *Book TV*, and more. She has appeared on hundreds of radio shows throughout the country; and her work has been featured on *The Dr. Laura Program*, *The Late Show with Stephen Colbert*, and *The Rush Limbaugh Show*. She is also the author of *The Alpha Female's Guide to Men and Marriage*.

Suzanne was born in St. Louis, Missouri, and graduated from Boston University in 1986. After ten years on the East Coast, Suzanne returned to the Midwest, where she now lives with her husband of eighteen years and their two teenagers.

www.suzannevenker.com
@suzannevenker